Bill Cosby

ENTERTAINER AND ACTIVIST

Black Americans of Achievement

LEGACY EDITION

Muhammad Ali

Maya Angelou

Josephine Baker

George Washington Carver

Ray Charles

Johnnie Cochran

Bill Cosby

Frederick Douglass

W.E.B. Du Bois

Jamie Foxx

Aretha Franklin

Marcus Garvey

Savion Glover

Alex Haley

Jimi Hendrix

Gregory Hines

Langston Hughes

Jesse Jackson

Magic Johnson

Scott Joplin

Coretta Scott King

Martin Luther King Jr.

Spike Lee

Malcolm X

Bob Marley

Thurgood Marshall

Barack Obama

Jesse Owens

Rosa Parks

Colin Powell

Condoleezza Rice

Chris Rock

Will Smith

Clarence Thomas

Sojourner Truth

Harriet Tubman

Nat Turner

Madam C.J. Walker

Booker T. Washington

Oprah Winfrey

Stevie Wonder

Tiger Woods

Bill Cosby

ENTERTAINER AND ACTIVIST

Sonya Kimble-Ellis

CHELSEA HOUSE
PUBLISHERS
An imprint of Infobase Publishing

Bill Cosby

Copyright © 2010 by Infobase Publishing

Chelsea House
An imprint of Infobase Publishing
132 West 31st Street
New York, NY 10001

Library of Congress Cataloging-in-Publication Data

Kimble-Ellis, Sonya.
Bill Cosby : entertainer and activist / by Sonya Kimble-Ellis.
   p.   cm. — (Black Americans of achievement, legacy edition)
Includes bibliographical references and index.
ISBN 978-1-60413-711-8 (hardcover)
1. Cosby, Bill, 1937—Juvenile literature. 2. Entertainers—United States—Biography—Juvenile literature. 3. Comedians—United States—Biography—Juvenile literature.
4. African American actors—Biography—Juvenile literature. I. Title.
PN2287.C632K56 2010
792.702'8092—dc22   [B]   2009050606

Text design by Keith Trego
Cover design by Keith Trego
Composition by Keith Trego
Cover printed by Bang Printing, Brainerd, Minn.
Book printed and bound by Bang Printing, Brainerd, Minn.
Date printed: July 2010
Printed in the United States of America

10 9 8 7 6 5 4 3 2 1

This book is printed on acid-free paper.

Contents

A Man of Many Firsts

It has been said that laughter is the sweetest sound. Yet for many entertainers, bringing smiles to the faces of millions is a difficult task. Comedian and entertainment icon Bill Cosby makes the process look easy. For decades, Cosby's comedy has been like music to the public's ears. He is a family-friendly comic who has attracted fans of all ages. While children love his playful charm, adults enjoy the comfortable way he pokes fun at daily life.

Early Cosby fans remember his stand-up routines on *The Tonight Show*. They also recall his Grammy-winning recordings *Bill Cosby Is a Very Funny Fellow Right!* and *I Started Out As a Child*, among others. He also won the hearts of television viewers with roles on *I Spy*, *The Cosby Show*, *Cosby*, and countless other programs. Young people instantly recognized him through his creation of the animated TV show *Fat Albert and the Cosby Kids*, the hit TV series *A Different World*, and appearances on signature Jell-O commercials. Cosby also lit up the silver screen in movies such as *Let's Do It Again*, *Uptown Saturday Night*, *A Piece of the Action*, and the concert film *Bill Cosby, Himself*.

An author, philanthropist, and educator, Bill Cosby has influences that are as diverse as his accomplishments. He credits comedians Jonathan Winters, Jack Benny, Buster Keaton, and the team of George Burns and Gracie Allen with helping to form his brand of comedy. Like artists in other disciplines, he often looked outside of his field for inspiration. He has said that the improvisational style of jazz musicians such as Dizzy Gillespie and Betty Carter helped him come up with new ways of crafting comedy routines. Oddly enough, he also was influenced by the humor and storytelling technique of author Mark Twain. He combined all of these elements to create a style that was uniquely Cosby.

Although he told a few race jokes early in his career, Bill Cosby's unique approach to comedy involved developing humor that did not include them. He felt audiences had become conditioned to hearing black comics performing that kind of humor. Edgy comedians, who sometimes used profanity, received lots of attention during Cosby's early days. He wanted no part of that either. Instead, Cosby based his routines on funny stories that were relatable to everyone. His tales revolved around his family, friends, and college days. Many of these stories fared better on some nights than others. When the jokes did not get laughs, he went back to the drawing board and spent hours coming up with ways to make his formula a success. The result was Cosby being the first of the popular African-American comedians to use "clean" jokes to get laughs.

Within no time, Cosby's laid-back demeanor and guy-next-door appeal made his stage shows memorable. During his routine, he usually sat center stage in a straight-back chair

Bill Cosby, second from right, cradles his Mark Twain award as he jokes with Malcolm-Jamal Warner, Phylicia Rashad, and Jerry Seinfeld at the conclusion of the Kennedy Center for the Performing Arts' fete for Cosby. He was honored with the center's annual Mark Twain Prize for American Humor on October 26, 2009.

with microphone in hand. The laughter he worked so hard to get during 3-minute sets at the start of his career eventually led to his developing 60- to 90-minute routines that sold out performances around the world.

In the book *Primetime Blues: African Americans on Network Television*, film historian Donald Bogle discussed Bill Cosby's persona in his early films, his comic style, and how he steered clear of cultural stereotypes:

> Watching Cosby . . . was seeing an expert comic technician in top form. While he didn't appear particularly spontane-ous, he was wholly natural with a timing so precise and proficient that he never missed a beat. In an era that saw a

proliferation of Black bucks in the movies, Cosby, without resorting to any of the old typing, sensitively presented the image of a relaxed working-class African American male. No dialect. No broken English. No outlandish exaggerations. No mugging.

Bogle goes on to add that, even though his audience knew Cosby was black, he was not looked upon as being "ethnic." Because he avoided stereotypes, Cosby was not placed into any specific cultural or racial box. "With his concerns about family and a bourgeois lifestyle," Bogle continued, "he seemed to be the embodiment of the cultural mainstream itself. Advertisers found him mainstream enough to hire him as a pitchman not only in Black publications, but in White ones as well and more significantly on network television."

Cosby's universal appeal began when he broke racial barriers as the first African-American actor to have a lead role in a dramatic series. The show was *I Spy*. It featured Cosby as one half of an undercover spy team that worked for the United States. Up until the creation of the show, most of the roles for blacks on television were not very complimentary. Cosby helped change that perception.

Of course, one of Cosby's greatest career achievements was his turn as TV dad Heathcliff "Cliff" Huxtable. In providing NBC with *The Cosby Show*, he presented the network with one

DID YOU KNOW?

Bill Cosby was the first African American to win an Emmy Award in the category of Outstanding Performance by an Actor in a Leading Role (Dramatic Series). The year was 1966; Cosby won for his work in the television drama *I Spy*. Gail Fisher was the first black female to win an Emmy (in 1970) for her role as Peggy Fair in the TV show *Mannix*.

of the highest-rated situation comedies (sitcoms) of all time. During its run, the sitcom was the most popular show in the Nielsen ratings for five consecutive seasons.

Cosby's appeal had its effect on other comics as well. Funny men like Eddie Murphy, Aries Spears, *Everybody Loves Raymond*'s Brad Garrett, and others have imitated Cosby's trademark body movements, voice, delivery, and laugh. In his documentary *Why We Laugh: Black Comedians on Black Comedy*, actor/filmmaker Robert Townsend discussed Cosby's impact. "Bill Cosby has always been in a league by himself," he said. "His superstardom came from the fact that he had a universal message."

Like many young people at the start of their careers, Bill Cosby struggled to find his footing. At first, he thought sports and then the military might be his roads to success. But after getting onstage one night at the suggestion of his friends, he knew he had found his calling. As a poor boy growing up in Philadelphia, he had no idea he would someday become a household name. He also had no clue that after dropping out of school, he would go on to earn several college degrees. The road, as he has often said, was not without bumps. But a lot can be learned from how he traveled from a simple life to superstardom. Ladies and gentlemen, introducing a very funny fellow—Bill Cosby!

2

Humble Beginnings

William Henry Cosby Jr. was born on July 12, 1937, in Philadelphia, Pennsylvania. His mother and father, Anna Pearl and William Cosby, were childhood sweethearts who were originally from Virginia. Like many African Americans of the era, the couple made their way North during the Great Depression of the 1930s to seek better economic opportunities. At that time, the United States and other parts of the world were suffering through a very severe economic slump. Bill Jr. was the oldest of four boys; his brothers were named James (who died of rheumatic fever at age six), Russell, and Robert.

Although it was difficult to find well-paying jobs, their parents worked extremely hard to take care of the family. Bill's father worked as a welder and his mother as a cleaning lady. The Cosbys lived in low-income, government-owned public housing, also known as the projects. Despite the fact that money was sometimes scarce, there was always food to eat and a roof over their heads. Since welding jobs were hard to come by, the elder Cosby took odd jobs whenever he could find them. When those dried up and he was unable to care for his family, he began drinking alcohol.

As his drinking became worse, William Sr. would leave home for days and weeks at a time. According to Bill, his father would disappear when the rent was due or right before Christmas. Forced to take matters into her own hands, Anna often worked as long as 12 hours a day. To lower their expenses, she moved the family to a smaller two-bedroom apartment.

In an effort to help make ends meet, Bill's father left home and joined the U.S. Navy. He worked aboard a ship as a mess steward. But the time spent at sea meant that he rarely saw his family. Every now and then, he sent money and saw Anna and the children when his ship docked at a nearby port. Eventually, though, Pop Cosby returned to his old ways. The checks in the mail stopped coming and so did Bill's dad. Intent on helping his mother take care of his brothers, Bill worked every type of job he could find. He shined shoes, worked in a grocery store, and sold fruit on the street.

Cosby credits his mother with shaping his career in those early days. At night, she read the boys Mark Twain, Jonathan Swift, and passages from the Bible. Cosby's grandfather, Samuel Russell Cosby, was also a big influence. On his official Web site, Cosby said of him, "My paternal grandfather told wonderful stories that were a combination of The Aesop Fables and The Bible, and the stories had humor, and that made me like him very much. Therefore, I made humor and storytelling parts of my personality." His grandfather's funny stories always had a moral about education or the importance of doing the right thing. He encouraged Bill to tell stories of his own. As a reward, he sometimes gave Bill some change to buy candy or some other treat. Bill's love of humor soon spilled over to his mother and brothers. As a young boy, he tried to make her laugh to get extra helpings of the sweets she had baked. Hoping to make their difficult home life easier, he used humor to make his brothers laugh too.

Radio was another way young Bill entertained himself. From the age of five, he spent many afternoons and evenings listening to comedians like Jonathan Winters, Jimmy Durante, and Jack Benny, who were very popular at the time. He also was intrigued by dramatic radio programs like *The Shadow, The Lone Ranger, Inner Sanctum,* and *Lights Out.* These radio programs, as well as later television programs like *The Colgate Comedy Hour,* helped influence his approach to comedy. It also gave him an early sense of storyline development as it related to radio and television shows.

In addition to entertaining his family, Bill used his comedic skills to make new friends and to get out of fights at school, which meant that he spent little time focusing his energy on schoolwork. In his book *Cosbyology: Essays and Observations from the Doctor of Comedy,* he wrote:

> I had a lot of fun in seventh grade. Except the thing called homework. Now I don't know what these people thought they were doing, but *homework*? It didn't make sense. If you work all day, why would you want to work when you come home? I figured it was just that old people wanted to annoy you.

Fortunately, Cosby's thoughts about education would change later in life.

But at the time, Bill had decided to drop out of school in the tenth grade. In 1956, he followed in his father's footsteps and joined the navy. While there, he took a correspondence course and obtained a high school diploma. During his stint in the military, he served as a medical corpsman at the Bethesda Naval Hospital in Maryland, where his responsibilities included helping with the physical rehabilitation of veterans of the Korean War (1950–1953). He also briefly worked aboard a ship that traveled from Newfoundland in Canada to Guantanamo Bay, Cuba.

SPORTS AND SEGREGATION

Cosby's love of athletics began in elementary school. His favorite events were the 100-yard (91.4 meters) dash, the triple jump, the high jump, and the discus and javelin throw. But track was not the only sport at which he excelled. During his time in the navy, he also played forward and guard on the National Naval Medical Center varsity basketball team. He found time to play on the football team and even tried out for the Baltimore Orioles baseball team.

It was during his travels to track meets across the country that Cosby first experienced racism. When making their way through the South, black members of the naval team were often made to enter restaurants through the back door. Once inside, they were allowed to eat their meals only in the kitchen and not with their teammates. Cosby had not experienced that kind of treatment growing up in the North. Though racism existed there, it was not as out in the open, so he saw little of it as a child.

For African Americans who lived in the South, however, life was much different. Because of Jim Crow laws—a system of state and local regulations that enforced total segregation of the races—blacks were not allowed to drink from the same water fountains as whites, could not use the same public restrooms, were forced to attend separate schools, and had to sit in separate movie theaters and concert halls. Sports were segregated too, but that began to change in 1947 when Jackie Robinson became the first black baseball player to play on the Brooklyn Dodgers, previously an all-white team. Two years later, he led the National League in batting averages and stolen bases. Prior to Robinson joining the Dodgers, blacks had played only in the Negro Leagues, a professional baseball league made up solely of African-American athletes. Over the next few years, sports such as tennis, boxing, and football all saw major accomplishments by black players.

These events paved the way for a number of civil rights milestones. On December 1, 1955, Rosa Parks was seated on a bus in Montgomery, Alabama. She had just left her job at a local department store and was on her way home. When a white passenger got on the bus and there were no more seats in the front, Parks and three other black passengers were asked to give up their seats. While the others got up, Parks refused

Jesse Owens

Jesse Owens broke racial barriers in his sport and in life. He was the first American athlete to win four gold medals at the Olympic Games. The feat was accomplished in Berlin, Germany, in 1936.

One of seven children, he was born James Cleveland Owens on September 12, 1913, in Oakville, Alabama. During the 1936 Olympic Games, Jesse leaped 26 feet (7.9 meters) and 5.25 inches (13.3 centimeters) in the long jump, setting a record that stood for 25 years. He also won the 100-meter (328 feet) dash in 10.3 seconds (which tied the world record), the 200-meter (656 ft) dash, and the 400-meter (1,312.3 ft) relay in 39.8 seconds (which set both Olympic and world records). With his medal wins, Owens disproved Adolf Hitler's theory that Aryans were a superior race.

After the Olympics, Owens dedicated his life to working with underprivileged children as a counselor and motivational speaker. He later worked as a board member and director of the Chicago Boys Club. He also acted as a consultant to the United States Olympic Committee. Later, he made goodwill visits to India and East Asia for the U.S. Department of State and worked as Secretary of the Illinois State Athletic Commission.

In 1976, President Gerald Ford presented Jesse Owens with the Medal of Freedom. Three years later, Owens visited the White House again to receive a Living Legend Award from President Jimmy Carter. Jesse Owens died on March 31, 1980 from lung cancer. After Owens' death, President George H.W. Bush presented his family with the Congressional Gold Medal in 1990.

In June 1936, Jesse Owens flies through the air during the long jump event at the Olympic Games in Berlin, Germany, where he won four gold medals. Adolf Hitler, the German dictator, famously left the stadium to avoid having to congratulate a black competitor.

to move and was arrested. This incident was a landmark event in what would become the civil rights movement. After Parks' arrest, the National Association for the Advancement of Colored People (NAACP) and Dr. Martin Luther King Jr. became involved and helped launch a boycott of buses in Montgomery. Nearly a year later, the U.S. Supreme Court ruled that buses there would be integrated.

Realizing that more work needed to be done to fight segregation, King led several sit-ins and marches over the next few years. The protests had an impact. On July 2, 1964, President Lyndon B. Johnson signed the Civil Rights Act, a bill that made it illegal for racial discrimination to occur in public places. In 1965, the Voting Rights Act was signed into law, allowing black Americans full and free access to the right to vote.

This was the world in which a young Bill Cosby was becoming a man, and it would help to shape his career as an entertainer, as it did for many African-American artists. Black entertainers of the era did their part to change the perception of blacks in America. They also spread the word about what was going on in the South. In their book *Hard Road to Freedom: The Story of African America*, authors James Oliver Horton and Lois E. Horton discussed the role and influence of entertainers during the Civil Rights era:

> Crossover music, the development of rock 'n' roll from its beginnings in rhythm and blues, and such early TV personalities as singers Nat "King" Cole and Eartha Kitt had given young white Americans glimpses of contemporary black culture. News coverage of civil rights demonstrations, however, brought black Americans and the violence of southern racism into American living rooms with a new immediacy and a kind of distant intimacy. Many young viewers were inspired by the courage of the demonstrators and the moral force of Martin Luther King as he urged his followers to speak truth to power.

COLLEGE OR COMEDY?

After completing his military service in 1960, Cosby was honorably discharged from the navy. By the time he left the military, his views on education had changed dramatically. He decided that pursuing a college degree could better his life and allow him to take care of his mother. So after winning a track scholarship to Philadelphia's Temple University, he settled on a major in physical education. While a student at Temple, Bill focused on class work and continued to excel in sports.

While getting an education was a top priority, Cosby also needed to earn money for books and general spending. He found a part-time job as a bartender at a club and got along famously with the customers. With a little encouragement from friends, he jumped on the club's small stage and began telling jokes. With each performance, the laughter from the audience grew and gave him even more confidence, so much so that he thought he might even have a chance at a career in entertainment.

To spread his wings, Cosby also performed at a small night-club called The Underground. His act was performed in one of the club's small rooms called The Cellar. He was paid $5 a night. Because the club did not have a stage, he created his own—propping up a chair on a table and then sitting down to deliver his jokes.

In order to jump-start his career, Cosby also teamed up with college buddy Herb Gart. The summer before Cosby's junior year at Temple, they discovered that the Gaslight Café in New York City was searching for new comics. With Gart acting as Cosby's manager, they took a trip to the club, where Cosby auditioned and was offered a job that lasted the entire summer. The schedule was grueling, with Cosby performing six sets a night. His schedule rotated with several singers who also had been hired. The acts performed from the time the Gaslight opened until it closed in the wee hours of the night.

For his efforts, Bill made $60 a week. He lived in a room over the Gaslight and the club's owner provided him with meals.

At times, Cosby performed in front of as few as five or six people. Undiscouraged, he used the opportunity to develop his stage show. He tried out a skit he called "The First Negro President." To stretch his set to 12 minutes, he borrowed a story, "The Down Home Players Do Julius Caesar," from a friend. Despite this foray into sketch comedy, he realized that an observational, storytelling brand of comedy was what he did best. After that summer, Bill Cosby decided to make a go of comedy full time.

As word spread about this young comic, Cosby began not only to earn more money, but also to develop a small following. Soon, he began receiving offers to tour other cities. In a 1963 interview on CBC-TV, he discussed his mindset at the time. On the one hand, he wanted to finish college. On the other, he could not resist the lure of comedy. He told the interviewer:

> That's when the trouble started. As a comic, I couldn't fully get the stage out of my mind. As a student, my grades fell. I was a pretty good student my first two years. Then my interest sort of dropped. And I figured the real reason I went to school was to get an education and if I kept going, I'd be doing myself a disservice. But I plan to go back.

So at the end of his junior year at Temple University, Bill Cosby left school and turned to comedy full time. His mother was not happy with his decision and made sure to let her son know how she felt. Even though Cosby assured her that he would become successful, he could not be certain that a major career in entertainment was beginning to take shape.

3

"I Want to Be a Comic"

By 1963, Bill Cosby's career in comedy was starting to come together. In the 1960s, a decade in which many now-famous comics were finding their voices, stage and television comedy was a developing phenomenon. Prior to that point, comedians were heard mostly on the radio or onstage. New York's Greenwich Village was a haven for comics. On any given night, patrons could catch a show featuring Flip Wilson, Joan Rivers, or Woody Allen. As an upcoming comedian, Cosby sometimes shared the same stage with these performers.

He began doing performances at clubs like The Bitter End and Café Wha?, two venues known for showcasing new talent. As he worked to make a name for himself, Cosby had a tough time standing out among several comedians who were known for using political and racial humor. Some of them did jokes that were filled with profanity. Cosby, however, would have none of that. His image was clean-cut. He dressed like a preppy college student, wearing button-down shirts and khaki pants. Sometimes he would don a collegiate sweater or jacket and tie.

Since there were few African-American comics at the time, Cosby often was compared to a politically charged entertainer named Dick Gregory, whose routines dealt with the racial tension of the period. Gregory started out playing small clubs in Chicago in the late 1950s. By 1961, Gregory had begun to make quite a name for himself and soon was playing larger clubs and making television appearances.

In an interview on Canadian television, Cosby said:

> If you want to compare myself and Dick Gregory, I'd say that it's not impossible. But would you compare Sid Caesar to Mort Sahl? No, you wouldn't do that. The only similarities we have are that we're both Negroes. I like to do different things. I like to move on my sets. The stage is a little small for me. I'd like to act. I'd like to write my own skits. This is the same way that Caesar works. I think Mort likes to sit in the same spot and talk about government and this is the way Dick works.

Cosby also had to contend with comparisons to African-American comics such as Redd Foxx, who had started his career in the early 1950s. Foxx was widely known for his profanity-laced brand of humor. Other black comics then on the rise included Godfrey Cambridge and a very young Richard Pryor.

Many would be surprised to find that there was one comedian in particular who caught Cosby's attention—Lenny Bruce. While Cosby was not influenced by Lenny Bruce's edgy material, he was impressed by the way Bruce performed the characters in his act. Cosby once said, "I went to see Lenny because I had all of his records, and the cuts that I enjoyed most had to do with human behavior."

Like most young comedians, Cosby experienced nights onstage that went well and others that did not. He used his bad experiences to learn how to handle hecklers and to find ways to rebound from jokes the crowd found unfunny. Early on, he sometimes slipped in a few one-liners about race to win over the audience. But those times were few and far between. When jokes fell flat, he got off the stage, sat at a table, and talked to patrons until he got a few laughs. Cosby wanted his jokes to revolve around stories he thought people of all races could relate to. It was at New York's Gaslight that he wrote and developed his popular routine "Noah and the Ark." It begins with a skeptical Noah sawing some wood in his rec room when God calls his name:

> [Cosby imitating a sawing sound] Whoompa, whoompa, whoompa, whoompa
> Noah!
> Somebody call?
> Whoompa, whoompa, whoompa
> Noah!
> Who is that?
> It's the Lord, Noah.
> Right! Where are ja? What you want? I've been good.
> I want you to build an Ark.
> Right! What's an Ark?
> Get some wood, build it 300 cubits by 80 cubits by 40 cubits—
> Right! What's a cubit?
> Let's see, a cubit . . . I used to know what a cubit was. Well, don't worry about that, Noah. When you get that done, go out into the world and collect all of the animals in the world by twos, male and female, and put them into the ark.
> Right! Who is this really?

The Noah routine, which became one of Cosby's signature pieces, continues in this way, with Noah being confused by all the things the Lord asks him to do. Throughout the routine, Noah wonders if someone is playing a joke on him.

As Cosby developed funnier routines and had more club appearances under his belt, he was able to command $200 per week. In those days, the amount was considered a very good salary. In an attempt to take his career to the next level, Cosby signed a management contract with Fred Weintraub, the owner of The Bitter End. One of Weintraub's staff managers, Roy Silver, was assigned to help him polish his routines. To accomplish that, they recorded each show and went over it line by line. They discussed his timing, which lines worked and which ones flopped. After rewriting some of the routines, Cosby practiced. He did this for several weeks and the end result was an impressive set that was 30 minutes long. As Cosby continued to play clubs on the East Coast, he soon found himself making as much as $500 a week. Feeling he was finally making progress, Cosby set his sights on even better paying gigs.

THE TONIGHT SHOW

Although the stage shows were coming along nicely, Cosby knew that television would give him a larger audience. For Cosby, though, there was just one hitch. He had done several auditions for *The Tonight Show*, then the biggest program on nighttime television. The opportunity to do a short routine on the show was every comic's dream. But he had tried out for the show three times and had not gotten a spot.

When approached by his manager to audition one last time, Cosby refused. He did not want to go to the set, present his routine, and get turned down yet again. It took Silver some time to convince Cosby to audition again. What Silver knew was that guest host Allan Sherman, who was also a comedian, was sitting in for regular host Johnny Carson. Cosby auditioned for Sherman that afternoon and was taping the show two hours later.

In 1963, during Cosby's first three-minute set on *The Tonight Show*, he talked about one of the things he knew

Bill Cosby performs on *The Ed Sullivan Show* in May 1964. Cosby's appearances here and on *The Tonight Show* helped expose him to national television audience.

best—television. He described how he loved but was frightened by monster movies as a child. But looking back on it, he said, he realized that because they were so slow, characters like Frankenstein's monster, the Mummy, and the Wolfman were not really all that scary. He also did a brief skit on Westerns, stagecoaches, and horses. Cosby's routine went over so well that he was asked back a second time. The appearances would prove to be a great boon to his career. After appearing on the show in 1965 with Johnny Carson, he got gigs headlining in clubs such as Mister Kelly's in Chicago, the Flamingo in Las Vegas, Hungry I in San Francisco, and Harrah's at Lake Tahoe. Before long he was being profiled in periodicals such as *Newsweek* and the *New York Times*.

Years later, as an established comedian, Cosby appeared on *The Tonight Show* and spoke to Johnny Carson about his first time on the show. "I walked out and was going to do my karate routine," he recalled.

> I hadn't really thought that it would be funny. I think people thought that as a black person, I would come out and talk about the back of the bus and the front of the restaurant and the side of the tree. I walked out and said I wanted to talk about karate. And they went, "Ha, ha!" I almost backed up and said, "What's so funny?" Then I went right into the routine.

FAMILY GUY

Bill Cosby's comedy career was not the only part of his life that was beginning to look bright. So was his love life. Around this time, he met Camille Hanks, a 19-year-old psychology

IN HIS OWN WORDS…

In his book *Fatherhood*, Bill Cosby described his relationship with his children: "We have shown all five of them constant attention, faith, and love. Like all parents since Adam and Eve (who never quite seemed to understand sibling rivalry), we have made mistakes; but we've learned from them, we've learned from the *kids*, and we've all grown together."

Bill Cosby and his wife, Camille, are photographed in New York City, on May 22, 1966, after he received an Emmy Award for his work on the television series, *I Spy*. Married since January 1964, the couple would have five children.

major at the University of Maryland. Camille and Bill were from different backgrounds. She grew up in a middle-class family in Silver Springs, Maryland, while he had lived in a poor neighborhood in Philadelphia. Mutual friends set up the couple on a blind date. At first, she was cautious about going out with a comedian. She had heard lots of unflattering stories about guys in the entertainment business. But after meeting him, she was taken by his charm and humor and decided to go on the date.

They married in January 1964 and eventually would have five children: Erika, Erinn, Ennis, Ensa, and Evin. Cosby once said they chose names that began with the letter E to represent excellence. During the course of his career, Cosby often used his family as material for jokes in his stage routine. They also were the basis for the Huxtable family on *The Cosby Show*. A strong believer in the importance of education, Camille Cosby went on obtain a doctorate in education from the University of Massachusetts in 1992.

Not one to rely solely on her husband's success, Camille became an educator and TV producer. She went on to co-produce the Tony Award–nominated *Having Our Say*, which won a Peabody Award for television in 1999, and another documentary titled *No Dreams Deferred*. She also was executive producer for the documentaries *Sylvia's Path* and *Ennis' Gift*. In addition, she wrote *Television's Imageable Influences: The Self-Perceptions of Young African Americans*, as well as several other books. Today, she and her husband have created several philanthropic foundations.

GET IT ON RECORD

Since Cosby was finding success on the stage and had gotten some television exposure, the next logical step in his career was to record a comedy album. His first LP, *Bill Cosby Is a Very Funny Fellow Right!*, was recorded at The Bitter End. The disk, released in 1963, contained his popular Noah skit. It was produced by Roy Silver and Allan Sherman, the man who had given him his first shot on *The Tonight Show*. Sherman wrote a glowing endorsement of Cosby on the back cover. Because Sherman had a following that trusted his judgment in talent, this tactic certainly helped boost the album's sales.

Cosby reportedly was paid $2,500 to sign with Warner Brothers Records—a decent sum of money in 1964. By industry standards, the album did not sell very well (under 10,000 copies), but the company decided to retain his contract. Later that year, Warner released his second comedy album, *I Started Out As a Child*. Although that record sold less than 9,000 copies, slow but consistent sales and belief in his talent prompted Warner Brothers to stick with their new find.

In the years that followed, Bill Cosby would have great success with his recordings. One of them—*Those of You With or Without Children, You'll Understand*—sold nearly a million copies after its release by Geffen Records in 1986. Of his more than 20 albums, the Recording Industry Association of America has certified 5 of Cosby's recordings platinum; 10 were certified gold. For his work he has received several Grammy Awards, three each in the categories of Best Comedy Performance and Best Comedy Recording. He also won two Grammys for Best Recording for Children.

TIME TO GET SERIOUS

Creativity was always one of Cosby's strong points. At the start of his career, he liked coming up with new ideas, skits, and characters. Most of these revolved around comedic stories. He had no idea, however, that dramatic acting on television was in his immediate future. During one of Cosby's shows in Pittsburg, California, comedian Carl Reiner was in the audience. Reiner went to see Cosby at the suggestion of his 16-year-old son, Rob, who had seen Cosby on *The Tonight Show*. After Reiner saw the show, he was convinced that Cosby was not only very funny, but that he had confidence and presence.

Reiner recommended Cosby to producer Sheldon Leonard, who was developing *I Spy*, an action-adventure television series about two American spies posing as a professional tennis player and his trainer. If the show was approved to go into production, it would be the first dramatic series to have a black actor as one of its stars. At first, the NBC network was hesitant to cast a little-known comic in the role. Convinced by Leonard, however, the NBC executives allowed the show to begin filming.

Leonard also was able to secure a big budget for *I Spy*, which helped the series live up to its action-adventure theme. He wanted the look of the show to be as realistic as possible. To that end, he made sure many of the episodes were filmed in exotic locations, such as Hong Kong, Spain, and Greece. When needed, however, they borrowed footage from news affiliates in Asia and elsewhere for background shots.

I Spy, which ran from 1965 to 1968, followed the exploits of spies Kelly Robinson (played by the late Robert Culp) and Alexander Scott (played by Cosby). Cosby's character was unusual for television at the time: He was a Rhodes scholar, a graduate of Temple University, and a sharp shooter and karate expert who spoke seven languages.

Initially, Cosby's character was supposed to be the bodyguard for Kelly Robinson. After meeting with the show's producers, it was decided that Cosby would not play sidekick to Culp's character. Their characters would be presented as equals. While the dramatic series addressed political problems of the day, Cosby also wanted to make sure that racial subjects—specifically the fact that he was black and Culp was white—would not be dealt with on the show.

Cosby, cast members, and producers waited nervously for reviews after the show's premiere. They knew it would be compared with other spy-themed entertainment of the era, such as the television series *The Man from U.N.C.L.E.* and *Get Smart*, as well as the James Bond film series. They worked to get stations to carry the show and to secure companies to air commercials as sponsors. Once *I Spy* aired, however, it received mixed reviews. A *New York Times* reporter said it needed style and attitude. Cosby himself admitted that his

Diahann Carroll

Actress/singer Diahann Carroll shared an important first with Bill Cosby. While he was the first black actor to appear on television with his role in the series *I Spy*, Carroll was the first black actress to star in her own television show, *Julia*. (The sitcom *Beulah*, which starred Ethel Waters, came first, but the character was featured in a stereotypical maid's role.)

Diahann Carroll was born Carol Diahann Johnson on July 17, 1935, in New York City. She made her debut on Broadway in 1954 in the play *The House of Flowers*. That same year, Carroll appeared in *Carmen Jones* alongside movie legends Dorothy Dandridge and Harry Belafonte.

Known as a beauty with class and style, Carroll got her big break in 1968 as the lead in her own NBC series titled *Julia*. In it, she played a nurse and single mom whose husband had died in the Vietnam War. For her work, she received a Golden Globe Award and an Emmy nomination for best actress. Like *I Spy*, Carroll's show was initially criticized for being unrealistic in its representation of a single black middle-class woman, but the enormously popular series was listed among the top 10 shows in 1969 and ran until 1971.

Since she had already endeared herself to fans, Carroll had no trouble winning over the public in her big-screen role for the film *Claudine*. The movie starred Carroll and James Earl Jones. As a welfare mother with six kids, her character was not as "glossy" as Julia and proved her versatility. She received an Oscar nomination for her efforts.

Ever intent on making a statement, Carroll approached executive producer Aaron Spelling in the mid-1980s about creating a role for her on his hit show *Dynasty*, because she felt the soap opera lacked a major African-American character with just as much power and money as everyone else on the show. The result was that Spelling created the role of Dominique Deveraux especially for her.

Carroll has made appearances on several television shows since *Dynasty*. Among the most memorable was her role as Whitley Gilbert's rich and clingy mom on *The Cosby Show* spin-off, *A Different World*. She is also the author of an autobiography, *The Legs are the Last to Go*.

performances in early episodes were stiff and not very good. He was a comedian, not a trained actor. But over time, he got used to working on a set in front of cameras. He also got better at delivering his lines and developing his cool but witty and charming character. A lot had been written in publications about costar Culp teaching Cosby how to act. This is something Culp adamantly denies. It was acting teacher Frank Silvera, Culp says, who helped Cosby hone his craft. Silvera came to the set, sat on the sidelines, and coached the young comedian during the early episodes.

Cosby and his costar got along very well. In a 2007 interview with The Archive of American Television (a project of the Academy of Television Arts & Sciences Foundation), Culp said of their relationship:

> Talent, that's me, recognizes genius instantly. I had seen it. I had seen the guy. I knew he was going to be terrific. . . . He trusted me totally, in regard to the story and all that it entailed, whether it was my writing or somebody else's writing. I entrusted him, obviously, about the comedy. The only time we stuck strictly to the script was when I wrote it. He never changed a syllable that I wrote. Because he assumed that I had eliminated all of the missteps, that those were the words that would tell the story in the shortest possible span. That was the basis of our professional working relationship. On top of everything else, we liked each other enormously.

It cannot be understated how groundbreaking *I Spy* was in its day. Prior to that series, African Americans were typically depicted in films as maids and butlers with little or no education. One of the most popular and controversial shows of all time was *Amos 'n' Andy*, which began as a radio program in the 1920s. In the radio version, white actors (and co-creators) Freeman Gosden and Charles Correll played the lead roles. Due to its popularity with radio audiences, *Amos 'n' Andy*

I Spy stars Bill Cosby and Robert Culp pose for a publicity photo during their show's initial run in 1960s. Although Cosby had no acting experience when he was cast on the show, Culp, a veteran actor, could immediately see the young comic's innate talent.

eventually debuted on CBS television in June 1951. This time, however, the series featured black actors Alvin Childress and Spencer Williams Jr. in the lead roles. The show lasted two seasons before being canceled. Some believe its cancellation occurred because of protests by the NAACP and many members of the black community, who did not approve of the stereotypical way Amos and Andy spoke and acted. Despite its controversy, *Amos 'n' Andy* is nevertheless regarded as pioneering because it was the first television show to have a predominantly African-American cast.

In Darryl Littleton's book, *Black Comedians on Black Comedy: How African-Americans Taught Us to Laugh*, comedian Dick Gregory offered his take on people seeing *Amos 'n' Andy* today: "I see nothing wrong with *Amos 'n' Andy* being on TV now, when you got other people you can look at. It's when you didn't have anything to look at but him and he represented us. . . . How [is] *Amos 'n' Andy* gonna damage us and we got a woman [Condoleezza Rice] Secretary of State?"

In the early years of radio and television, there were African-American actors who had less controversial roles, but most of them were still stereotypical. In the late 1930s, Ethel Waters, an actress who appeared on radio and Broadway, starred as a maid in the show *Beulah*. Another actress, Amanda Randolph, played the housekeeper Louise on *Make Room for Daddy*, a television sitcom that starred comedian Danny Thomas. Eddie "Rochester" Anderson worked as Jack Benny's comedy sidekick, first on his radio show and later on his television series and in films.

Still, the importance of these early African-American characters cannot be dismissed. They did, in fact, make it easier for others who followed. They helped lay the foundation for a new representation of blacks in the coming years, a representation that Cosby himself would exemplify. In his book *Primetime Blues: African Americans on Network Television*, film historian Donald Bogle wrote:

Looking back on these early servant characters, one might want to dismiss all of them. Yet the Black actors and actresses of these early series enlivened television with a different type of style and presence. Their dialects, double takes . . . their body language were all cultural signs that energized the early series, sometimes giving them an edge, sometimes spicing up otherwise routine and bland material.

I Spy changed the course of television and set a precedent for blacks in dramatic roles on the small screen. With hard work, Cosby and Culp won over fans and critics and created a television drama still held in high esteem today. (In fact, *I Spy* was so popular that a reunion television movie aired in 1994.) During the show's initial run, Cosby won three Emmy Awards for Best Male Actor in a Dramatic Television Series. For each of the show's three seasons, it was among the top 20 popular shows on television. As much as *I Spy* was groundbreaking for African Americans in general, it also gave Bill Cosby the kind of clout he needed for all the television and film roles that were yet to come.

4

Cosby's Turn on Television

The success of *I Spy* gave Bill Cosby a great deal of leverage. He had proven he could be appealing to TV-viewing audiences, and his stage shows and recordings demonstrated his popularity. His income was also beginning to reflect his accomplishments. He was now playing Las Vegas hot spots like Harrah's and was able to buy a home for his wife and children, as well as one for his mother.

A year after *I Spy* ended its run, Cosby worked out a deal with NBC that would have been the envy of any comedian or actor. Under the agreement, he received a contract that would allow him to develop his own television series, cartoons, and variety shows. During this time, Cosby's manager also had begun negotiating a movie contract with Warner Brothers.

Developing characters that were relatable to viewers was one of Cosby's top priorities. Before filming began on *The Bill Cosby Show* in 1969, he had discussions with network executives about

Bill Cosby in character as a high school teacher and coach on *The Bill Cosby Show*, which lasted from 1969 to 1971. It was the first time a black actor starred in his own eponymous television series.

his character's line of work. NBC thought the lead character in the situation comedy should be a detective, but Cosby wanted him to be a teacher. He was also hesitant about the show being just for laughs. His character, Chet Kincaid, had to be a real person who dealt with real problems—his own as well as those of his students. As a result, Kincaid was introduced to viewers as a physical education teacher, a career choice Cosby had almost made earlier on in life.

Kincaid taught at Richard Allen Holmes High School in Los Angeles. In each episode, he had interactions with his students, school staff, and members of his family. While some critics criticized the show for being boring, others loved it. Cosby also used the show as an opportunity to cast veteran African-American comics like Jackie "Moms" Mabley and Mantan Moreland. Although the show met with mixed reviews, *The Bill Cosby Show* has been credited as the inspiration for other successful shows of its type, such as *The White Shadow. The Bill Cosby Show* ran until 1971.

While Cosby was making inroads on sitcom television, he was also making changes behind the scenes. His show provided opportunities for blacks who wanted to work on TV crews and gave actors another place to spotlight their talents. Several episodes of *The Bill Cosby Show* featured casts comprised almost entirely of African-American actors.

Soon after his sitcom ended, Cosby tried his hand at variety. An hour-long show produced by George Schlatter (the same man who created the funny and cutting-edge variety show *Laugh In*), *The New Bill Cosby Show* aired in September 1972 and featured skits, songs, and dance. Guest stars on the variety show included Harry Belafonte, Lily Tomlin, Sidney Poitier, the Smothers Brothers, Groucho Marx, Richard Pryor, and other top acts.

IN HIS OWN WORDS...

In a 1963 interview on Canadian television, Bill Cosby said, "Every comic starts out because he's funny at parties, makes his friends laugh and is the clown. So I went out and tried to draw up things about what people really feel."

Flip Wilson

The first widely successful African-American host of a television variety show, Flip Wilson (whose real first name was Clerow) was born on December 8, 1933, in Jersey City, New Jersey. One of 18 children, he was raised mostly in foster homes and spent time in a reform school.

It was in the air force that he earned the name Flip. He became popular among the other servicemen for his funny stories and impressions. They thought he had a "flipped out" way of telling jokes. The name stuck. But more importantly, Wilson got the opportunity to travel to other bases to do comedy shows for other military men. After leaving the air force at age 21, he worked odd jobs and performed at local comedy clubs. As his popularity grew, he secured a spot at the popular Apollo Theater and began work on a comedy album.

As a result of the buzz, Wilson was able to win an appearance on *The Tonight Show*. The audience loved him and, as a result, he got steady work with guest-spot appearances on popular shows like *The Ed Sullivan Show*; *Love, American Style*; and *Rowan & Martin's Laugh-in*. He would appear on *The Tonight Show* more than 25 times.

In September 1970, he hit it big with his own NBC variety program called *The Flip Wilson Show*. During its run, the show transcended racial barriers and had guests ranging from James Brown, Lena Horne, and Sammy Davis Jr. to singer Bobby Darin, football legend Joe Namath, and comedian George Carlin. On the show, Wilson became known for his funny characters, including Reverend Leroy and Geraldine, whose often-imitated lines were "What you see is what you get" and "The devil made me do it." Geraldine's signature look was big hair, miniskirts, heels, and colorful dresses. In fact, Wilson's influence for playing a female character can be seen in the work of comedians Jamie Foxx, Martin Lawrence, and Tyler Perry.

The Flip Wilson Show was broadcast until June 1974. During its run, it won two Emmy Awards in 1971 for Best Variety Show and Best Writing In A Variety Show. Wilson also received a Golden Globe Award for Best Actor in a Television Series in 1970. While he did not find the same kind of success later in his career, he did appear in *Uptown Saturday Night* with Cosby in 1974 and had roles in two films, *The Fish That Saved Pittsburgh* and *Skatetown USA*, in 1979. In 1984, he worked for one season on the television show *People Are Funny*. He also starred in *Charlie & Co.*, a television sitcom about a middle-class family living in Chicago. It costarred Gladys Knight and aired for two seasons. He also made several guest-spot television appearances in the 1990s.

Flip Wilson died of liver cancer on November 25, 1998.

One of Cosby's most enduring creations is the Saturday morning cartoon series, *Fat Albert and the Cosby Kids*, which first ran on NBC from 1972 to 1985. Shown at center, Rudy, and clockwise from top, Fat Albert, Weird Harold, Bill Cosby, Bucky, Russell, Mushmouth, and Dumb Donald.

Mushmouth, Russell, Weird Harold, Dumb Donald, Weasel, and Bucky.

At the start of each episode, Cosby appeared standing in a junkyard that was partially animated. Holding a paintbrush, he tossed props back and forth to animated Cosby kids as the theme music played along. Cosby's opening line was always the same: "This is Bill Cosby comin' at you with music and fun, and if you're not careful you may learn something before it's done. So let's get ready, okay? Hey, hey, hey!"

Much of the show came from Cosby's own childhood experiences or was based on his stand-up routines. In one episode, the characters Bill and Russell (named for Cosby and his brother) end up in the hospital. The episode was inspired by a bit Cosby used in his routine about having his tonsils taken out. Another show revolved around Fat Albert not being allowed to play in a game because of his weight. In addition to silly shenanigans, the series also dealt with serious topics such as sexually transmitted diseases, peer pressure, and race. When it came to those aspects of the show, the network kept Gordon Berry, a professor of education at the University of California, Los Angeles (UCLA), on hand as an educational consultant.

The Fat Albert cartoons would run for 12 seasons, with the last five years of the series filming under the name *The New Fat Albert Show*. In those later episodes, the names and looks of some of the characters were changed. Some characters were dropped entirely. The show was enormously popular during its run and produced a variety of spin-offs, including comic books, children's books, and lunch boxes. Cosby even gave the U.S. Department of Health and Human Services permission to use his characters for a comic book that talked about the dangers of alcohol.

Talk of making a live-action Fat Albert movie began in 1993. A little-known actor was found to take on the lead role, but the studio lost interest in the project. Eight years later, in 2001, Cosby co-wrote a script and hired actor Forest Whitaker to direct. When creative differences between Whitaker and Cosby arose, Joel Zwick was brought in to take over the reigns. Zwick had directed many comedies. Among them were *Laverne & Shirley*, *Full House*, *Webster*, *Hangin' with Mr. Cooper*, and

Family Matters. Best of all, Cosby liked the fact that Zwick had experience working with young actors.

Actor Kenan Thompson, who had been seen on such shows as *Kenan & Kel* and *Saturday Night Live,* played Fat Albert. Released in December 2004, *Fat Albert* mixed live action with animation, with the gang coming out of the cartoon world into the real world. In order to make the transition, Cosby breathed new life into some of the characters: Dumb Donald finally removed his hat and became smart, and Mushmouth learned to speak properly. The film earned mixed reviews from critics, and many fans felt that Fat Albert and the gang should have remained a cartoon.

WORKING WITH KIDS

Cosby loved working on Fat Albert because he loved to entertain and teach children. In order to continue to work with children, he lent his talents to *Electric Company,* a PBS program designed to help develop the reading skills of kids between the ages of 6 and 10. Through song and humor, stars such as Morgan Freeman, Rita Moreno, Judy Graubart, Lee Chamberlin, and Skip Hinnant taught children vowel sounds, spelling techniques, and new words. The show, which began airing in 1971, also featured cartoons and sing-alongs. Cosby liked the direction the show took in educating kids and did not mind the low salary or the long hours the episodes sometimes took to film. Although the education aspect of the show was carefully developed, Cosby ad-libbed some of his spots when he felt the script was not working as written. Between 1971 and 1973, he appeared in more than 250 episodes as the character Hank.

A POPULAR PITCHMAN

Beginning in the 1970s, Cosby capitalized on his popularity by starring in a string of television commercials. As one of the first black spokesmen for major products, Cosby used his charm to convince the public to buy everything from cars and cameras to beverages and food. Before his run as a product pitchman, there were only a handful of African Americans who had been associated with major products, and few black faces appeared in advertising.

One of the most famous African-American pitchpeople of the late 1800s and early 1900s was "Aunt Jemima," a character who appeared on the front of the popular pancake ready-mix that was first developed in 1889. Two years later, an actress named Nancy Green was hired as the manufacturer's spokeswoman. While many people believed the recipe was Green's, it was not. Despite this, her face became one of the world's most recognizable advertising trademarks. For her part, Green was given a lifetime contract with the company and traveled across the country promoting the product. In fact, before Green joined the Aunt Jemima Manufacturing Company, it was struggling to survive. After she became its spokeswoman, pancake flour sales were up and people were eating pancakes at all times of the day, not just for breakfast. When Green died, two other women were hired to promote the mix. In 1989, Aunt Jemima's image on the box was updated. Her headscarf was removed and she was given pearl earrings and a dress with a lace collar.

Decades later, black entertainers like Cosby were hired specifically to promote products, a clear indication of just how far African Americans had come. Some of Cosby's most famous commercials were for Jell-O. He promoted the company's entire line, including Jell-O Gelatin Pops, Jell-O Pudding, and Jell-O Pudding Pops. In one commercial, he sat at a table with Jell-O pudding in front of him, looked into the camera, and said: "Dinner's just been served and the kid will stare at the plate and ask what's for dessert? And you answer Jell-O pudding and suddenly your child loves broccoli. Jell-O pudding. You can't be a child without it!"

Cosby's Jell-O commercials were numerous. In another, he and a group of kids were seated at a long formal table, with everyone dressed in tuxedos, smiling and eating Jell-O Jigglers. In yet another commercial, he sat on the steps with two kids, eating pudding with them. Cosby casually asked when they last had pudding, as they scooped their small dishes clear of the dessert. Then, he turned to the camera and playfully pleaded with moms to make more Jell-O pudding for the kids.

In a 1989 commercial for Coca-Cola, Cosby found a way to bring his love of jazz onto the screen. Set on a dark soundstage meant to represent a jazz club, late jazz singer Betty Carter sang the theme song "Can't Beat the Feeling" while Cosby played all the instruments behind her. He momentarily took a break from playing the piano, downed a few gulps of Coca-Cola, and resumed the jam session. Cosby has also been a pitchman for Kodak, the Ford Motor Company, Texas Instruments, Dutch Masters, and E.F. Hutton.

AND AN AUTHOR, TOO

Because Cosby thinks of himself as an all-around entertainer, he has always been ready to take on new challenges. He has even had a successful career as an author and has written more than 15 books. One of his most famous books, *Father-hood*, was published in 1986. It spent 54 weeks on the *New York Times* bestseller list. Several of his later books, including *Time Flies* and *I Am What I Ate . . . and I'm Frightened!!!*, were bestsellers as well. The popular Little Bill book series continues to be a hit with children. Published by Scholastic, these beginning-reader books deal with issues that are important to youngsters.

5

Guerilla Filmmaking

Even though he had planned on doing more television projects, Cosby felt the time had come to try his hand at films. He saw filmmaking as his next logical move, but initially he had a few false starts. First, he was considered for a movie being developed by Francis Ford Coppola, best known as the director of the Godfather film series. Cosby was excited about the prospect of working with such a respected director. But scheduling conflicts and Cosby's eventual split with his manager halted the project. Although several other scripts came across his desk, Cosby had trouble securing those roles. The top brass at movie companies were hesitant to take a chance on someone without a proven track record in films.

Despite all the rejections, Cosby was determined to get a movie off the ground. With encouragement from his wife, he decided to use his own money to make a film. He put together a film crew and headed to Arizona to begin filming *Man and Boy*. A family-oriented story set in the Old West, the movie follows the struggles of Caleb (played by Cosby) and his family after Caleb's son takes off on the family's horse, their most prized possession, and it is later stolen. *Man and Boy* followed their adventures as they went off to find the horse. Bill spent well over $300,000 to get the project completed.

Man and Boy was eventually released on a limited number of screens in 1972. Reviews were somewhat encouraging for such a small film that had no major movie machine backing it. Reviewing the film for the *New York Times* on March 16, 1972, Howard Thompson wrote:

> The plight of a black man in the frontier West is a wonderfully provocative film theme. As the star and engineer of an admirably economic project, *Man and Boy*, which genuinely tries to say something worthwhile, Bill Cosby is to be commended. If only the picture were better. The material is here. . . . Pulled together taut and hard, along with some good, cutting dialogue, the film might have scored a neat homerun. But at least it puts Mr. Cosby on first base in screen drama.

As Cosby was trying to get his film career off the ground, he was also working on his doctoral degree from the University of Massachusetts. He was allowed to use his work and research on the Fat Albert series as part of his studies. He handed in scripts from the show, and his professors evaluated the techniques Cosby used in combining education and entertainment. His doctorate dissertation was called *An Integration of the Visual Media Via "Fat Albert and the Cosby Kids" into the Elementary School Curriculum as a Teaching Aid and Vehicle to Achieve Increased Learning* and was published in 1976. Since earning his degree, the comedian has received many honorary degrees from a number of universities.

While he continued managing his film production company and getting ready for new projects, Cosby heard from his old *I Spy* buddy and costar Robert Culp, who had gotten hold of a script about two private eyes. This time, he and Cosby would not be playing slick worldly spies; instead their characters would be detectives who were down on their luck. Directed by Culp, the 1972 film *Hickey & Boggs* was by no means a big hit, but their fans from the *I Spy* days went out to the theaters to see the pair back in action. Yet the release of *Hickey & Boggs* served an important purpose—it kept Cosby's face on the big screen at a time when studios were still not ready to bank on him.

A CONTROVERSIAL ERA IN FILMMAKING

In the early 1970s, Bill Cosby was not the only talented African American trying to make a mark in the film industry. Many young black actors and directors were producing films at the time that a new genre of filmmaking, called blaxploitation, was becoming very popular. More than 200 such movies were released before the genre's popularity faded in the early 1980s. While some blaxploitation films received backing from major film companies, others were made by smaller production houses. Nevertheless, they were a cultural phenomenon.

Before the blaxploitation era, few African-American actors and actresses beyond such esteemed performers like Sidney Poitier could get roles other than maids, butlers, or sidekicks to their white counterparts. Blaxploitation helped to change that. In these films, blacks existed primarily within their own world. They made lots of money, carried guns, and lived life on their own terms. Despite these films' success, Cosby and organizations such as the NAACP had problems with what they saw as the films' glorification of drug dealers and a fast-paced lifestyle. Such criticisms aside, the public went to see blaxploitation films in record numbers. This helped the film-makers, movie companies, and several actors make a good deal of money. In the 2002 documentary *Baadasssss Cinema*, film critic Armond White addressed the contradictions of the era: "Black audiences in the '70s [were] indeed . . . politically conscious . . . but too often, going to those movies, you were encouraged to simply forget the politics and indulge the cars, the clothes, the drugs."

The blaxploitation era began with the 1971 release of Melvin Van Peebles' cutting-edge film *Sweet Sweetback's Baadasssss Song*. Funded mostly with Van Peebles' own money, the movie was the first black-themed picture to achieve box-office success by Hollywood standards. Van Peebles' successful film was followed by many other films in which an African-American man was the main hero. Among the most successful of these were the Shaft films, two of which were directed by photographer and filmmaker Gordon Parks. Starring actor Richard Roundtree as Shaft, the trilogy includes *Shaft* (1971), *Shaft's Big Score* (1972), and *Shaft in Africa* (1973). Another Shaft film was made in 2000, starring Samuel L. Jackson in the lead as the nephew of the original Shaft.

Other popular blaxploitation films included *Superfly T.N.T.* and *The Mack*, both released in 1973. Their themes revolved around guns, drugs, pimps, and ladies of the night. Other types of themes explored during the era included horror, romance, and robbery. A popular female actress who emerged from the genre was Pam Grier. As a pistol-carrying no-nonsense woman, she represented the beautiful female who was independent and could take care of herself. Grier starred in *Coffy*, *Foxy Brown*, and a string of other movies. She has been acknowledged for paving the way for other actresses in the genre. Well after the blaxploitation period was over, director Quentin Tarantino was credited with reviving Grier's career. He wrote and directed the cult film *Jackie Brown* in 1997, with Grier as the star.

In the *Baadasssss* documentary, actor Samuel L. Jackson described the intent of movie companies during the height of blaxploitation:

It just meant that they had found a way to tap into a black audience. And just exploit the dollars that they had by making movies for them, by them, that are about them. It didn't mean that they were exploiting our sensibilities or anything else. They were just trying to make a dollar. . . . We needed something to make us feel better about ourselves. We watched the news every day. People were being beat down. Things weren't progressing the way we wanted them to. Martin Luther King had asked us to do one thing. Stokely Carmichael and Rap Brown were asking us to do another thing. The Panthers were doing their thing. The power movement and the films were a spin-off of these things.

The blaxploitation genre was not, however, all about crime and drugs. Several films released during that time explored another side of black life. *The Spook Who Sat by the Door*, based on a book by Sam Greenlee, was about a CIA employee who was secretly a black nationalist. There were even blaxploitation martial arts movies such as *T.N.T. Jackson* and *Black Belt Jones*.

COSBY'S FILM CONTRIBUTIONS

Uncomfortable with the blaxploitation films, Cosby made a special effort to appear in films that could be seen by his family and fans. The goal was made much easier when he teamed up with actor Sidney Poitier. A pioneer in his own right, Poitier was directing several family-based films comprised of mostly African-American casts.

In 1974, the two men, along with veteran actor and civil rights advocate Harry Belafonte, appeared in *Uptown Saturday Night*. Acting in the lead roles, Poitier and Cosby starred as a factory worker and his buddy who get tangled up with gangsters over a winning lottery ticket. Belafonte played a mock Marlon Brando–type gangster. *Uptown* also featured a cameo appearance by Richard Pryor. During filming, over 1,000 blacks were hired as crew members, cast, and extras. The result of Cosby's and Poitier's efforts was a successful film that did well with black and white audiences alike. A *Los Angeles Times* reviewer called it "one of the year's most enjoyable movies. The old-fashioned kind that leaves you feeling good all over."

The hit-making duo next appeared in *Let's Do It Again.* By the time this movie was released in 1976, the face of television was beginning to change. Shows with mostly or all-black casts, such as *The Jeffersons, Good Times,* and *Sanford and Son,* were being viewed in homes across the country in record numbers. The success of Cosby and Poitier's first movie and the changing climate of the entertainment industry were reflected in the amount of money they received for the second. For the second film, Poitier was given a larger budget of $2.5 million. In addition to Cosby and Poitier, *Let's Do It Again* starred Ossie Davis, Jimmie Walker, and John Amos. Denise Nicholas, who later starred in the TV version of the Poitier film *In the Heat of the Night,* played Cosby's wife.

In the film, Cosby's and Poitier's characters were members of a lodge that had plans to build a day-care center. To try to double the lodge's money, the guys take the cash to Las Vegas to try and double it. Breaking box office records when it opened, *Let's Do It Again* earned $64,000 during its three-day opening weekend. Not overwhelming by today's standards, the amount was impressive for the mid-1970s. (The film's title song, sung by The Staple Singers, became a huge hit as well. The group also sang most of the songs used in the Diahann Carroll and James Earl Jones movie *Claudine.*)

Next came *A Piece of the Action* (1977), in which Cosby and Poitier starred as thieves who had never been caught in the act. When they are finally caught, rather than spend time in jail, the two reluctantly go to work at a youth center for troubled teens. They get more than they bargain for when they end up becoming attached to the kids. This film also hit a home run at the box office.

Above, Bill Cosby and Sidney Poitier are seen in their 1974 film, *Uptown Saturday Night*. The duo would team up again in *Let's Do It Again* (1975) and *A Piece of the Action* (1977).

While creating the string of winners with Poitier, Cosby set out to make movies on his own. In 1976, he worked with Raquel Welch and Harvey Keitel on the film *Mother, Jugs & Speed*. In this movie about ambulance paramedics, Cosby played Mother, the best driver at F&B Ambulance Service, a fun-loving guy who liked to listen to music and drink beer. Antics ensued as the crew competed with larger ambulance companies to get to the scene of the distress calls first. *California Suite*, a 1978 comedy by Neil Simon, was Cosby's

(continues on page 50)

Sidney Poitier

One of the world's first international African-American film stars, Sidney Poitier began his acting career in the 1950s. The youngest of seven children, he was born in Miami, Florida, on February 20, 1927, and grew up in a small village in the Bahamas. His family, originally from the Bahamas, moved back to the island when he was eleven.

At age 16, Poitier came to New York City with just three dollars in his pocket. Once there, he briefly served in the U.S. Army and worked as a dishwasher. Needing to earn more money, he responded to a newspaper advertisement that sought actors. He had no experience but went to the audition for the American Negro Theatre.

Because of his lack of schooling, he was barely able to read the script. Ashamed and humiliated, he vowed to get better, both at reading and at acting. He returned six months later, auditioned, and became an official member of the company. His first role was in the play *Days of Our Youth*, in which he was the understudy for Harry Belafonte. Afterward, Sidney appeared in 10 more plays with the company.

At age 22, Poitier acted in his first movie, *No Way Out*, which marked the beginning of an illustrious career. A graceful and elegant man, Poitier has been credited with choosing roles that showed blacks in positive ways that had never been seen on film before. His movie credits include *Cry, the Beloved Country* (1952), *Blackboard Jungle* (1955), and *A Patch of Blue* (1965). Some of his signature roles include his work in Lorraine Hansberry's *A Raisin in the Sun* (1961), in which he played Walter Lee Younger, and *To Sir, with Love* (1967), in which he portrayed a teacher and mentor to British high school students. Also released in 1967 was *In the Heat of the Night*, in which he played a police detective from up north investigating a murder in a Southern town. When the script called for a white actor to slap him, Poitier insisted that he be able to slap him in return to show their equality.

As an actor and director, Poitier had a string of hits in the 1970s in films that costarred Bill Cosby and Harry Belafonte. He also directed the successful Gene Wilder and Richard Pryor film *Stir Crazy* (1980). For his contributions to film, he has received numerous awards. In 1963, he became the first African-American male to win an Academy Award for Best Actor for his work in *Lilies of the Field*. Sidney Poitier's biography is titled *The Measure of a Man: A Spiritual Autobiography*.

In an interview on *The Oprah Winfrey Show*, Poitier summed up his experience as a successful black actor:

I knew that this color was my color, but I had no idea that it was a condemnation of me. It was going to stand in the way of my expressing myself in life as a human being. So when I had to face it, I decided that those who thought of me in such negative terms, I was going to lay down a challenge. No, I am not going to try to be as good as you; I'm going to set my standards higher, and I will be better!

Actor Sidney Poitier appears with Lilia Skala in a scene from the 1963 film *Lilies of the Field*. Poitier won an Academy Award for his role as Homer Smith.

(continued from page 47)

next gig. The all-star cast included Jane Fonda, Alan Alda, Richard Pryor, and Walter Matthau. In 1981, he starred in the poorly received Disney film *The Devil and Max Devlin*. Even though this film met with a lukewarm reception, he hit pay dirt when he decided to return to what he knew best. In 1983, he wrote and directed a film of his concert performance in Toronto, Canada, *Bill Cosby: Himself.* Throughout his comedy routine, Cosby talked about everything from raising and feeding children to dentists and weekend adventures. The movie featured the family-oriented style of humor that always had brought him success.

Cosby returned to his law-enforcement-character roots in 1987, playing a secret agent in *Leonard Part 6*. Its theme was farfetched: He portrayed an ex-spy asked by the CIA to help stop an evil force from brainwashing small animals into killing people. While the movie tanked at the box office, his 1990 follow-up, *Ghost Dad*, did slightly better, although critics had difficulty with the film's hard-to-believe premise: Cosby played a father who tried to communicate with his children after his death. Of Cosby's difficulty to recapture his earlier film success, in 1988 a *New York Times* reporter wrote:

> Mr. Cosby is not the only television star to stumble in attempting a crossover to the movies. The film careers of both Tom Selleck (*Magnum, P.I.*) and Ted Danson (*Cheers*) were strewn with duds before they both finally connected in the current hit *Three Men and a Baby*. No book heads the

DID YOU KNOW?

Bill Cosby received America's highest civilian honor, the Presidential Medal of Freedom, in July 2002.

best-seller lists forever. Mr. Cosby's efforts, at best pieces of pleasant fluff, had an impressive run for the money.

Most critics and fans agree that Cosby's film career peaked early on and the huge success he longed for in that arena never came. The small screen, however, is where Bill Cosby would make his biggest impact and would far surpass whatever success he had ever imagined.

6

America's Favorite Dad

Throughout his career, Bill Cosby always liked to have several irons in the fire at once. Although he worked on a number of films throughout the 1980s, he was ready to star in another television series. Still, Cosby was unhappy with the shoot-'em-up shows he saw on television. It was important to him to not only steer away from violence, but also to steer clear of anything that was stereotypical or showed women in an unflattering light.

A creative person who never takes off his thinking cap, Cosby was always coming up with new ideas and jotting them down. In a 2009 interview with *Like It Is* host Gil Noble, Cosby described his process and reason for coming up with what would become his smash-hit sitcom *The Cosby Show*:

> It came from my monologues. I decided that I wanted
> to do a television series. I was very tired of watching TV

shows where little kids were smarter than the adults and they were cracking jokes on the adults. I wanted to take the house back. My wife didn't like the idea I had about the guy being a chauffer with his own business and his wife being a plumber. So then we decided on making them a doctor and lawyer. The whole idea behind their professions is that these two people are doing what they love, and they worked so hard through their academics. They were loving and taking on the challenge of educating themselves and their children.

Initially, Cosby approached ABC about his sitcom idea. The network turned down the series. Luckily for him, however, Brandon Tartikoff, the head of programming at NBC, happened to catch one of his monologues on *The Tonight Show*. Tartikoff thought Cosby would be great to star in a sitcom. But there was a catch. It had been nearly eight years since Cosby appeared in a weekly show, and with the exception of *I Spy*, he had not achieved top ratings success with any of his other shows. And at the time, situation comedies were not a hot commodity. Citing those reasons, NBC gave Tartikoff some resistance.

Undeterred, Tartikoff asked the production team of Marcy Carsey and Tom Werner to develop the series with Cosby. Once it was put together, Tartikoff and network president Grant Tinker gave them the go-ahead to shoot seven episodes. *The Cosby Show*, as it was eventually tagged, was set to feature Bill as Dr. Heathcliff Huxtable, his wife, Clair, and their five children.

THE CHANGING FACE OF SITCOMS

Although no African-American sitcoms would match the enormous popularity of *The Cosby Show*, it was preceded by a number of important black sitcoms in the 1970s that helped pave the way for its success. Among them was *Good Times*, a show that revolved around a Chicago family with financial hardships. The Evans family was a loving household with two parents who supported their children. The family members were James (John Amos), Florida (Esther Rolle), J.J. (Jimmie Walker), Thelma (Bern Nadette Stanis), and Michael (Ralph Carter). The cast also included neighbor Willona Woods (Ja'Net Dubois) and Penny (Janet Jackson). Other notable African-American family television shows of the era included *What's Happening!!* and *That's My Mama.*

The Cosby Show made its way onto television just as another black sitcom, *The Jeffersons,* was about to leave the air. One of several spin-offs of the hit comedy *All in the Family, The Jeffersons* had debuted in 1975 and lasted until 1985. On *The Jeffersons,* George Jefferson (played by Sherman Hemsley) was a successful businessman who owned several dry cleaners. The show revolved around him and his wife, Louise, played by Isabel Sanford. They lived in an upscale apartment in New York City. Unlike Bill Cosby's character on *The Cosby Show,* George was brash and did not hold his tongue, but he often met his match with his wife or with their wisecracking maid Florence (played by Marla Gibbs). George also butted heads with his white neighbors but still managed to reveal some lovable qualities that won over viewers. Fans of the show and members of the cast were saddened that the series was canceled without a final farewell episode.

COSBY RULES!

The Cosby Show began its first season on September 20, 1984. From almost the first episode, Thursday nights at 8:00 P.M. became an event in millions of households across the United States.

Cosby wanted to ensure that the scripts were family friendly and socially and psychologically sound. To accomplish that goal, he used much of his family experience and routines from his comedy act as material for the show. The network also hired Harvard professor Dr. Alvin F. Poussaint as a consultant.

More than anything else, Cosby wanted the characters that would populate his series to be admirable people.

The Huxtables lived in a brownstone in Brooklyn, New York. Cosby's character, Cliff, was a obstetrician/gynecologist who maintained a practice on the ground floor, and Clair, played by theater actress Phylicia Rashad, was a lawyer. The couple's kids included Denise, a quirky teenager, played by Lisa Bonet. On the show, she wore eccentric clothes and unique hairstyles. Malcolm-Jamal Warner portrayed Theo, the family's only son. Theo spent lots of time teasing his younger sisters, Vanessa and Rudy, played by Tempestt Bledsoe and Keisha Knight Pulliam. Eldest sister Sondra, acted by Yale School of Drama graduate Sabrina Le Beauf, rounded out the cast. On the show, her character attended Princeton University and married her male-chauvinist-turned-sweetheart husband, Elvin Tibideaux, who was played by Geoffrey Owens. The two later had twins, named Nelson and Winnie after the Mandelas of South Africa. Denise would marry Martin Kendall, played by actor Joseph C. Phillips, who already had a daughter, Olivia, from a previous marriage. She was portrayed by Raven-Symoné, who would go on to have her own show, *That's So Raven.*

In the show's later seasons, other characters were introduced, including cousin Pam, played by Erika Alexander. Erika went on to play sassy lawyer Maxine on *Living Single* and to act in several television shows. Carl Anthony Payne played Cockroach, Theo's best friend. A host of other memorable actors, including Earle Hyman who played the children's grandfather, also appeared on the show. During the series, Cosby got the opportunity to bring in musical guest stars like Stevie Wonder, Patti LaBelle, Dizzy Gillespie, Lena Horne, and Sammy Davis Jr. Up-and-coming actors such as Angela Bassett, Blair Underwood, Robin Givens, and Alicia Keys snagged small acting spots on the show.

While *The Cosby Show* was an ensemble series, Cosby was undoubtedly the show's highlight. His work on the show would

Phylicia Rashad, as Clair Huxtable, talks on the telephone while Bill Cosby, as Dr. Cliff Huxtable, and other cast members of *The Cosby Show* look on during the taping of the sitcom's final episode in New York City, on March 6, 1992. From left clockwise are Rashad; Clarice Taylor as Anna Huxtable; Cosby; Earl Hyman as Russell Huxtable; Deon Richmond as Rudy's best friend Kenny, partially hidden; Malcolm-Jamal Warner as Theo; Keshia Knight Pulliam as Rudy; and Raven-Symoné as Olivia.

eventually label him as "America's Favorite Dad," because his character represented the cool but concerned parent. He was no-nonsense but liked to have fun. And his signature brightly colored sweaters became almost as popular as the man who wore them. In the documentary *Why We Laugh*, comedian Bill Bellamy said of *The Cosby Show*: "The color just erased. They became just a family. The next thing you know, Bill Cosby is America's favorite dad . . . a Black guy. So it didn't matter about his color. The essence is what it's all about."

While there were many memorable episodes of the show, a few stick out to longtime fans: the family funeral for Rudy's dead fish; Theo trying to impress a girl by wearing a knockoff of an expensive shirt made by sister Denise; Rudy having her friends over for a slumber party while Cliff gives them hysterical horse rides on his knee; Vanessa getting engaged to a guy she has not introduced to the family; Clair discovering a marijuana joint in Theo's textbook; the family lip-synching the Ray Charles song "(Night Time Is) The Right Time" to their grandparents for an anniversary; and the Huxtables turning the household into the real world to show Theo how tough it is to be an adult.

When it first aired, *The Cosby Show* was criticized for being unrealistic and not representative of the majority of African-American families. In response, Cosby argued that his show represented middle-class black families who really did exist; viewers just had not previously seen them on television. In his book *Primetime Blues: African Americans on Network Television*, Donald Bogle wrote: "What struck me most about *The Cosby Show* was that I had seen, during my suburban childhood, African American families similar to the Huxtables. But I had never seen such a family on television."

Continuing in his own defense, Cosby was quick to point out that the show did address racial issues and several episodes discussed the history of civil rights in America. In one episode, Theo used his grandparents' memories to write a paper about the 1963 March on Washington. In another, Rudy and the family end the show by sitting on the living room couch watching a rebroadcast of Dr. Martin Luther King Jr.'s "I Have a Dream" speech.

Throughout its run, *The Cosby Show* was beloved by millions. A ratings success, it was third in the ratings in its first season and was the most popular show in America for four consecutive seasons after that, which meant that it was an enormous moneymaker for NBC. The network charged $110,000 for 30-second-spot commercials during the first season. By season two, that amount was pushed up to $200,000. Just prior to the end of the series, the going rate for such commercials aired during the show was close to $400,000. In 1986, Cosby earned $22 million when he sold reruns rights to WWOR for three and a half years. And *The Cosby Show* remains popular: It is still shown in syndication today on TV Land and other networks.

Phylicia Rashad and other cast members often have discussed the show's popularity. In an interview from the The Archive of American Television (Academy of Television Arts & Sciences Foundation), Rashad said:

> What Bill did, in being authentic, was to show that people are more alike than we could ever be different. You don't have to pretend to be other than you are. Just be authentically human. People respond to that. I've received letters from young girls who said they wanted to be lawyers because of what they had seen. I would encounter people in airports who would have the most sincere expressions of gratitude for having saved a marriage or for ways to deal with their children.

In addition to being commercially successful, the show also won several Emmy Awards for Outstanding Comedy Series and a Golden Globe. But by the early 1990s, the show began to slip in the ratings and was being surpassed by comedies like *Roseanne* and *Married . . . with Children*, sitcoms that centered on working-class families. *The Cosby Show*'s last season was in 1992. The final episode was Theo's graduation from college, a fitting end to a character that had been diagnosed with dyslexia during the show's run. In the *Chicago Tribune*, William Raspberry described the series' impact:

> *The Cosby Show* has taped its last episode and, after April 30, will be reduced to reruns. But what a show it has been!

It has entertained us, of course. But it has also educated us, sensitized us, induced us to introspection and perhaps, during its eight-year run, even helped bring us together across the divides of race and class.... Well, it did more than just survive. For most of its run, it was at or near the very top of the ratings. The "Huxtables," Cosby's TV household, became a part of the language with which we discuss family—alongside *Ozzie and Harriet* and *Father Knows*

Phylicia Rashad

Best known as the lovable mom on *The Cosby Show*, Phylicia Rashad initially made her mark as a dramatic stage actress. She also endeared herself to audiences with her performance in the 2004 revival of the play *A Raisin in the Sun*. For her inspired performance, she became the first African-American woman to win a Tony Award in the best actress category.

Born in Harris County, Texas, Phylicia Rashad is the older sister of director, choreographer, and actress Debbie Allen. Her older brother, Andrew, is a musician. Rashad decided on an acting career early in life. She received a bachelor's degree in Fine Arts from Howard University, from which she graduated with honors. She came to New York in the early 1970s and began acting with the esteemed Negro Ensemble Company. Her first major gig came in 1975, playing a Munchkin in the stage production of *The Wiz*. She was also the understudy for the roles of Dorothy and Glinda the Good Witch. Next came work in 1981 as the understudy for the role of Deena in the hit Broadway musical *Dreamgirls*. After leaving the show a year later, she snagged a recurring part on the daytime soap opera *One Life to Live*.

A few years later, she auditioned for Bill Cosby and got the role of his TV wife, Clair Huxtable, on *The Cosby Show*. For eight seasons, she portrayed a confident lawyer who took care of her family. Several years later, she played Cosby's wife again on the sitcom *Cosby*, which ran from 1996 to 2000. When the latter show's run was complete, she returned to the stage. In addition to appearing in the stage production of *A Raisin in the Sun*, she reprised the role in a made-for-television special. She later appeared in the Broadway stage productions of *Cymbeline*, *Gem of the Ocean*, *Cat on a Hot Tin Roof*, and *August: Osage County*.

Best. The Cosby Show became, for a time, a Thursday-night addiction. And not just among white people, who, it was said, could enjoy it without having to examine their own psyches for latent racism. Not just among amnesiac middle-class blacks, who, as the accusation had it, were grateful for a show that allowed them to disidentify with their blackness. Not even just among Americans. As I learned on a visit to South Africa, blacks and whites in that unlikely place loved *The Cosby Show.*

An interesting side note to the show's success is the fact that, toward the end of the show's run, it was rumored that NBC was for sale. Cosby expressed interest in buying the network and went so far as to meet with his lawyer to outline the specifics of such a purchase. He also spoke to individuals about becoming partners in the purchase. Norman Brokaw, his agent, met with network president Robert C. Wright to discuss Cosby's interest. At the end of the meeting, however, Wright said NBC was not for sale. During the highly publicized talks, other parties, including Paramount Communications, were said to have been interested in buying NBC. The rumored asking price was as much as $4 billion. Cosby's net worth at the time was close to $300 million.

A DIFFERENT WORLD

Cosby's television winning streak continued when he decided to produce a spin-off titled *A Different World*. It aired in the 8:30 P.M. slot right after *The Cosby Show*. The success of *The Cosby Show* gave him the opportunity to produce a show that dealt with young people and education. Initially, the show was supposed to focus on Denise Huxtable and her experiences at a fictitious school, Hillman College. The series was a perfect vehicle for Lisa Bonet.

In addition to Denise, the show's major players during the first season were Jaleesa, a divorcée portrayed by Dawnn Lewis,

Shown here are Kadeem Hardison, as Dwayne Wayne, and Lisa Bonet, as Denise Huxtable, in a scene from a first season episode of *A Different World*.

who also co-wrote the show's theme song; Maggie, an offbeat free spirit played by Marisa Tomei; Dwayne Wayne, played by Kadeem Hardison; Southern belle Whitley Gilbert, portrayed by Jasmine Guy; and womanizing, irresponsible Ron Johnson, played by Darryl Bell. It became clear early in the first season that Guy's Whitley character was a favorite among viewers. Whitley was quick-witted, funny, and unashamed of her rich background, even when teased by her peers.

Instead of focusing on the kids and their classroom studies, most of the episodes revolved around dormitory life and romance issues. Some episodes dealt with career decisions and study habits. During one of the series' later episodes, a student discovers a room at the college that once was used as a hiding place during the Underground Railroad—an informal network of secret routes and safe houses used by abolitionists to help slaves escape to free states and Canada in the years before the Civil War (1861–1865).

During Bonet's time on the show, her character struggled with her grades and in finding a career path. By the second season, her character was absent from the show. Questions remain as to why Bonet left the show. Some have said the move was a result of Cosby's unhappiness with her decision to do a nude love scene in a movie called *Angel Heart*. The role was a departure for a clean-cut Cosby kid and Cosby did not want the image he had built to be tarnished. It also has been said that she left *A Different World* due to her pregnancy. Nevertheless, Bonet returned to *The Cosby Show* in 1989 and remained until the show's end.

Several years into the series, Debbie Allen was brought in to direct and revamp *A Different World*. In addition to the comedy that viewers had become accustomed to, more serious issues were added to certain episodes. Of the show's serious themes, Alice La Deane wrote in the *L.A. Times* in 1992:

> In the course of the past year, *A Different World* has presented fully-dimensional, objective and even painful consideration of such real-world concerns as AIDS, date rape, scholastic application, affirmative action, the cons as well as the pros of the Gulf intervention and sexual responsibility. In fact . . . this series dealt with so brave a subject as black self-perception and self-esteem, considering some delicate realities which are rarely addressed on deep-thought hour shows, much less sitcoms.

In addition to doing well in the ratings, the show was even credited with boosting college enrollment. *A Different World* would enjoy six successful seasons and would prove that Cosby could be as successful a television producer as he was a comedian.

AFTER THE HUXTABLES

Once *The Cosby Show* concluded, Cosby worked on several other television programs. On *The Cosby Mysteries* (1994–1995), he portrayed Guy Hanks, a New York forensic expert and criminologist. A retiree from the police force after winning a $44 million lottery, Hanks was often called upon for help by one of his old partners, played by James Naughton. The series also starred Lynn Whitfield and rapper/actor Mos Def. The show was canceled after just 18 episodes aired on NBC. The storyline seemed a bit disjointed and the network never gave Cosby the opportunity to work out the kinks.

Bill also fell short with *Kids Say the Darndest Things* and *You Bet Your Life*. He fared better with *Cosby*, a new sitcom that began in 1996. In it, he played Hilton Lucas, an airline worker who was laid off from his job. Left without much to do in his spare time, he drives his wife, daughter, and neighbors crazy because of his boredom. When the show was being put together, actress/singer Telma Hopkins was hired to play Hilton's wife, Ruthie. When the producers felt the on-screen chemistry did not work, they paired him with his old on-screen wife, Phylicia Rashad.

Though he was happy about working with Rashad again, Cosby wanted to make sure the characters were not just retreads of Cliff and Clair. Based on a British comedy titled *One Foot in the Grave*, the original idea for the show called for Hilton to be gruff and angry at the world. Cosby came up with a character that was a bit friendlier. Hilton's day consisted of hanging out in his wife's café and interacting with neighbors. Comic relief was added by comedian Doug E. Doug, who played their upstairs neighbor, Griffin. The cast was rounded out with Madeline Kahn, who played Ruthie's best friend, Pauline; and T'Keyah Keymáh, best known for her work on *In Living Color*, as their daughter, Erica. While not able to duplicate the incredible success of *The Cosby Show*, *Cosby* lasted four seasons and helped to cement Bill Cosby's legacy as a television giant.

7

Trying Times

The year was 1997. Just a few years earlier, Bill Cosby had finished his run at the helm of one of TV's most successful sitcoms. Now, he was in the midst of his CBS sitcom, *Cosby*. Little did he know that the year would be filled with heartache and scandal. While on set, Cosby received a call that would be any parent's worst nightmare.

On January 16, 1997, his 27-year-old son, Ennis, was killed. It happened in the wee hours of the morning. Ennis was changing a flat tire on an off-ramp of a San Diego highway. Police believed someone was trying to rob him and things went terribly wrong. A report on the incident from CNN.com read:

> Robbery was the apparent motive for the attack, according to investigators, although nothing appears to have been taken. Investigators say there is a witness to at least some of the incident. A police spokesman described Bill Cosby as

"extremely upset" but "very coherent" when he was told of his son's death.

During the search for the man who committed the crime, Cosby asked that the press not focus on the fact that the offender was white. He also expressed his dismay over the fact that the press showed photos of his son's body at the crime scene. As it turned out, a 19-year-old Ukrainian man, Mikhail Markhasev, was ultimately charged with the crime. He has since been sentenced to life imprisonment.

Several years after the incident, the convicted killer appealed the decision, but the appeal was later withdrawn. In a written statement, he apologized to the Cosby family, admitted his guilt, and said it was time to do the right thing. In a statement released to the press, Cosby said: "Our hearts go out to each and every family that such an incident occurs to. This is a life experience that's truly difficult to share."

As the story unfolded on the news, the public learned that many traits of Theo's character on *The Cosby Show* were modeled after Ennis. As a child, Ennis was dyslexic but overcame his disability. After graduating from Morehouse College, he set out on a career of working with people who had learning challenges that were much like his own. Tall, handsome, and hard working, Ennis was Cosby's only son and he made his father very proud. Before this tragic turn of events, Ennis was due to return to school to complete his doctorate degree at Teachers College at Columbia University.

To honor his son's memory, Cosby created the Hello Friend/Ennis William Cosby Foundation. (The foundation's name is taken from how Ennis typically greeted someone: "Hello Friend.") The foundation provides a place for teachers to find information about strategies designed to help youngsters with learning challenges. In addition, students of Fordham University's Graduate School of Education, called Cosby Scholars, receive training in early detection. (When Ennis was

A photo of Bill Cosby's son, Ennis, taken in New York City, on June 15, 1996. Ennis Cosby was murdered on January 16, 1997.

a young boy, not much was known about dyslexia, so his condition went undiagnosed for some time.) Hello Friend also has an online tutoring program on the foundation's Web site: www.hellofriend.org.

In the March/April 2008 issue of *Haute Living*, Cosby's daughter Erika wrote an article, "Hello Friend," in which she discussed her brother and his challenges:

> Though he was taken from us too soon, he lived long enough to discover his passion for teaching, a triumph for him after a lifetime struggle with dyslexia. Ennis eventually discovered, through proper instruction, that he was not slow or incapable of learning, but simply put, he learned and comprehended differently from others. In an excerpt from a paper he wrote titled "Teaching from the Heart," he states: "How will my experience influence change in the school system? I am soon to be a teacher who can influence change by my experiences as a victim of the system. I believe that if more teachers are aware of the signs of dyslexia and learning disabilities in the class, then fewer students like me will slip through the cracks of the system."

Shortly after Ennis was killed, Cosby and his family were dealt another blow: Cosby was accused of fathering a child out of wedlock. A 22-year-old woman named Autumn Jackson claimed to be his illegitimate daughter. She privately asked Cosby to give her $40 million to remain quiet about the scandal. She threatened to give the information to *The Globe*, a tabloid newspaper, and even went so far as to contact the executives of some of the companies that Cosby endorsed. His lawyers contacted the authorities about the extortion attempt and the information was made public. While Cosby admitted that he was guilty of having an affair, he said Autumn was not his daughter.

After arriving in New York to try to get money from Cosby's lawyer, she was arrested. She was tried in federal court and found guilty of extortion. For months, the entire incident and court proceedings were played out in the media. During the trial, Cosby testified that 20 years prior, he had paid Autumn's mother $100,000 to keep the brief affair quiet. Cosby also said he paid for Autumn's college tuition, bought her a car, helped her out financially, and set up a trust fund for her. While he did not claim her as his daughter, he also admitted that he had never taken a paternity test. He feared that if the news got out, it would ruin his reputation. The question remained: If Cosby had been helping Autumn financially, why the sudden extortion effort? According to Cosby, things got tense between them when Autumn dropped out of school and he failed to return any of her calls. He also said his wife, Camille, had learned of the affair many years before the trial. Jackson served 14 months of a 26-month sentence.

Although long known as America's Favorite Dad, Cosby has not always had a smooth relationship with his children. His daughter Erinn had trouble with substance abuse during the 1980s, and his relationship with her during this period could best be described as "rocky." It became that way after she admitted she often used cocaine and marijuana. Because he did not feel she was trustworthy, Cosby distanced himself from her while she worked through her problems. He was quoted in the *National Enquirer* as having said at the time: "We love her and want her to get better, but we have to take a very firm, very tough stand that forces her to realize that no one can fix things for her. She has to beat this on her own." In 1992, Erinn claimed she had to fight off boxer Mike Tyson when he made sexual advances toward her.

AIRING DIRTY LAUNDRY

With tragedy and scandal surrounding him, Bill Cosby entered the new century rather quietly. But a speech he gave in May

2004 changed all of that. The event was a gala held in Constitution Hall in Washington, D.C. The occasion marked the fiftieth anniversary of the *Brown v. Board of Education* Supreme Court decision, which declared racial segregation in schools and other public places to be illegal. The landmark case would not only dismantle Jim Crow laws across the nation, but it also helped to spur on the civil rights movement.

During Cosby's talk at the fiftieth anniversary celebration, he criticized poor African Americans' parenting skills, use of slang and foul language, acceptance of juvenile delinquency and drop-out rates, and more. During his speech, he said:

> They're standing on the corner and they can't speak English. I can't even talk the way these people talk: "Why you ain't," "Where you is." . . . And I blamed the kid until I heard the mother talk. And then I heard the father talk. . . . People marched and were hit in the face with rocks to get an education, and now we've got these knuckleheads walking around. The lower economic people are not holding up their end in this deal. These people are not parenting. . . . Brown or black versus the Board of Education is no longer the white person's problem. We have got to take the neighborhood back.

Cosby's comments upset many in the African-American community who felt he was airing black America's dirty laundry in public and was feeding into negative racial stereotypes. Others believed he should have also taken aim at society for its contributions to the problems. Still, there were people who not only agreed with his comments but felt his speech was an opportunity to open up positive dialogue. Because his comments caused a media frenzy, Cosby did several television, newspaper, and radio interviews to defend his views.

Firm in his beliefs, Cosby did not back down. He was intent on getting his point across. During a panel session at an

Education Forum in the Washington, D.C., he scolded parents who did not take any interest in their kids' homework. He also took them to task for managing their children with their cell phones. Although Cosby acknowledged that racism is still a problem in America, he stressed that good parenting would help black children deal with it—and the responsibilities of life—much better.

Among Cosby's critics was the professor and writer Michael Eric Dyson. He agreed that the speech had some good points. Dyson felt, however, that the way Cosby stated these points reinforced racial stereotypes. Dyson felt so strongly about Cosby's comments that he penned a book about it, *Is Bill Cosby Right?: Or Has The Middle Class Lost Its Mind?* In the book and in interviews, Dyson claimed Cosby was a rich and powerful black American who looked down on the poor. Dyson also suggested that Cosby did not acknowledge the unbalanced school systems in rich and middle-class schools versus poor schools. While certain schools have state-of-the-art technology and big operating budgets, poorer schools are struggling to survive. In the text, Dyson also came down on Cosby for not being more active during the civil rights era and in avoiding race issues throughout his career:

> He has famously demurred in his duties as a racial repre-
> sentative. He has flatly refused over the years to deal with
> blackness and color in his comedy. Cosby was defensive,
> even defiant, in his views, as prickly a racial avoider as
> one might imagine for a man who traded so brilliantly on
> dimensions of black culture in his comedy. While Cosby
> took full advantage of the civil rights struggle, he reso-
> lutely denied it a seat at his artistic table. Thus it's hard to
> swallow Cosby's flailing away at youth for neglecting their
> history, and overlooking the gains paid for by the blood
> of their ancestors, when he reneged on its service when
> it beckoned at his door. It is ironic that Cosby has finally

Bill Cosby *(center)* speaks as Alvin F. Poussaint *(left)* and moderator Tim Russert *(right)* look on during a taping of *Meet the Press* on October 14, 2007. Cosby and Poussaint went on the program to discuss their book *Come On, People: On the Path from Victims to Victors.*

answered the call to racial leadership forty years after it might have made a constructive difference. But it is downright tragic that he should use his perch to lob rhetorical bombs at the poor.

While some agreed with Dyson, others came to Cosby's defense. In *Time*, Phylicia Rashad said:

What he's addressing specifically, and this is true for our nation, is that education is not valued the way it needs to be for the sake of our young people and our nation. And I think he's right about that. Teachers are not held in the same regard as they were when I was in school. He's not wrong about that, and he's right for asserting that parents have to advocate for their children.

Another Cosby supporter was the director Spike Lee. In 2004, Lee received a lifetime achievement award at an event in Dallas, Texas. During his acceptance speech, he echoed Cosby's ideas. "We have to get back to stressing education because this gangster rap stuff is taking us down the wrong area," he stated. "We have young black children growing up thinking that if you get straight A's, act intelligent and try to get good grades, that somehow they're acting white or that they're a sellout. . . . People jumped on Bill Cosby, but he wasn't lying."

Taking up his own defense, Cosby wrote a response that clearly outlined his position. In Cosby's book *Come On, People: On The Path From Victims to Victors*, co-written with Dr. Alvin F. Poussaint, Cosby provides messages of personal responsibility, inspirational anecdotes, and tips for overcoming adversity. Important talking points in the book include taking care of one's health and children, organizing communities, combating violence, and growing into prosperity. In the text, the co-authors outline why they wrote the book:

IN HIS OWN WORDS...

During an interview with Gil Noble on *Like It Is* in 2009, Bill Cosby stated:

I said in 2004, our children are trying to tell us something and we're not listening. Some people decided to leave that part out. They said that some of the things I said were harsh, that it didn't have any substance, that i didn't like poor people. So I said let me go out and talk to the people and show them what I'm talking about. I went to churches and neighborhoods to talk to people to make it clear.

The reason we wrote this book was in the hope that it can help your kids brighten the world too. Every last one of our children is gifted in some way. It's just that no one has helped each of them discover and nurture his or her own particular gift.

Without inspiration and guidance, these gifted children can make decisions that are absolutely, incredibly dumb. We know that many of you are as old as we are and some of you are just as confused. You, too, wonder how a young person can say, "I'm not gonna flip burgers, so I might as well go out and sell drugs. And if I get killed, I get killed." Now that boggles our minds, because we didn't come from that. We came from survival. And we want our youngsters to learn as quickly as possible what we learned the slow, hard way.

Although many people remain divided over the issue Cosby brought to the public's attention and many, like Dyson, argue that Cosby chose the "safe" route to celebrity, it is also clear that Bill Cosby has used his celebrity to do good for those who were less fortunate. This is most recently exemplified by his founding of the Hello Friend foundation. His contributions to the black community should not be measured only by his political stances or his career choices, but also by his positive influence as a role model.

8

Leaving a Legacy

Most artists want to create work that will last long after they are gone. Bill Cosby has done just that—created television programs, films, books, and recordings that will keep his legacy alive for years to come. But that's not all.

Bill Cosby's philanthropic work is just as impressive. It has always been his belief that his wealth should be used to help others. Over the years, Bill and Camille Cosby have contributed privately to charities and social service organizations, as well as paid for the college education of several students.

Their most widely publicized contribution is perhaps their $20 million donation to Spelman College, a black women's college in Atlanta, Georgia, in 1988. It was the largest donation ever made by an individual to a historically African-American college. It was also one of the biggest donations ever made to a single school. Every year, *Giving USA* keeps track of charitable donations that surpass $1 million. The book's author, Nathan Weber, writes that the Cosbys' contribution ranked as the fourth-highest contribution by an individual to an educational institution.

At an inauguration dinner honoring the school president, Johnnetta B. Cole, Cosby stated, "Mrs. Cosby and I have been blessed because I found a vein of gold in the side of a mountain." He went on to explain that the donation was out of the couple's love and respect for the college and challenged other celebrities to contribute to deserving schools as well. According to Cole, most of the generous gift was used to build a new academic center that included women's and audio-visual centers, classrooms for the college's honors program, and faculty offices. The building was named the Camille Olivia Hanks Cosby Academic Center, after Cosby's wife. The Cosbys' daughter Erinn is a graduate of Spelman.

But their contributions to universities did not stop with Spelman. The Cosbys also split $3.1 million among several colleges at once: Fisk University, Howard University, Florida A&M, and Shaw University. In addition, Cosby reportedly gave $325,000 to Central State University and has maintained a relationship with the school. In recent years, he did several free concerts at the school. The performances were based on an agreement that the university would, in turn, raise a certain amount to benefit the school. In June 2006, Morehouse School

IN HIS OWN WORDS...

On the Gil Noble show *Like It Is*, Bill Cosby said: "It's the community service that's important. I believe that we should teach and encourage our children to get involved; whether it's the Boys & Girls Club, Salvation Army, the Red Cross, or the church in the neighborhood."

of Medicine in Atlanta also benefited from the Cosbys' gener-
osity. The couple gave the school $3 million. The money was
used to further the study of mental health.

FOR ART'S SAKE

Throughout his career, Bill Cosby also has helped other artists
complete projects. In 1970, director Melvin Van Peebles started
his career by directing the controversial film *Watermelon Man*.
The Columbia movie was about a prejudiced white insurance
executive (played by black actor Godfrey Cambridge) who
wakes up one day and discovers that he is African American.
Forced to embrace his new identity, he eventually becomes a
revolutionary. The film was moderately successful, taking in a
little more than $1.5 million. It was made in 22 days and cost
just under $1 million to make.

Cosby also funded Van Peebles' second effort, *Sweet
Sweetback's Baadasssss Song*. Van Peebles used money he
earned from *Watermelon Man* for financing, but to meet the
film's $500,000 budget, Van Peebles borrowed $50,000 from
none other than Bill Cosby. *Sweet Sweetback* was released in
1971 and became the groundbreaking film that ushered in
the blaxploitation film era. It grossed over $4 million at the
box office.

Van Peebles was not the only filmmaker Cosby helped to
complete a film. Cosby, along with other celebrities, helped
with the completion of Spike Lee's 1992 film *Malcolm X*.
The movie was based on *The Autobiography of Malcolm X*, a
book written by Alex Haley. When Lee proposed adapting the
book to film, there already had been several failed attempts
at making a movie about Malcolm X. Some of them included
scripts that did not work and public disagreements over who
should direct.

Much of the difficulty in getting a film made about Malcolm
X was the fact that he was a controversial figure during the civil

Spike Lee is pictured at the twentieth anniversary screening of his film *Do The Right Thing* in New York City, on June 29, 2009. When Lee needed money to complete the filming of his movie *Malcolm X*, Cosby helped to finance it.

rights era. Unlike Dr. Martin Luther King Jr., who advocated gaining racial equality through nonviolent means, Malcolm X offered another view on racial equality. When asked if he supported using violence to achieve equality, he said, "It doesn't mean that I advocate violence, but at the same time, I am not against using violence in self-defense. I don't call it violence when it's self-defense, I call it intelligence." Born in Omaha, Nebraska, on May 19, 1925, he was originally named Malcolm Little. After spending part of his life involved in gambling, drugs, and other illegal activities, he went to jail, but he later reformed after becoming a member of the Nation of Islam. As a civil rights leader, Malcolm said: "We declare our right on this earth . . . to be a human being, to be respected as a human being, to be given the rights of a human being in this society, on this earth, in this day, which we intend to bring into existence by any means necessary."

When executives at Warner Brothers finally approved *Malcolm X*, the company budgeted $28 million for the film. Director Spike Lee used some of his own money to meet costs. But when the film company would not give him any more cash, he came up with an alternative. During a speech in San Francisco, California, in June 1996, Lee recalled:

> At the top of my list was Bill Cosby. I called up Bill Cosby and went through a few pleasantries, asked him how Camille was, his wife—and once he heard that he said, "Spike, how much do you need?" Since Bill Cosby was the first on a long list, I didn't want to be greedy, and tempt the gods, so when he asked how much, I gave Bill the low number. He said, "Tell me who to make the check out to and you can pick it up from my accountant's office tomorrow." I took the subway into Manhattan, got the check, and ran to the bank and deposited it. We were very happy about that.

Spike continued calling celebrities to get the movie made, including Oprah Winfrey, Magic Johnson, Michael Jordan, Prince, and Janet Jackson. According to Lee, they all wrote six-figure checks, which helped with the movie's completion. These were "checks that they could not use as tax write-offs, . . . but just so we could get the film into the theaters the way we wanted to," Lee remarked. "They all came through." After the film was released in 1992, *Malcolm X* brought in over $48 million during its box-office run.

INFLUENCING OTHERS

Cosby is probably one of the most imitated and respected comedians in the world. Everyone from fans to entertainers has offered up a version of his voice, laugh, and physicality. Imitators have posted their Cosby impersonations on video Web sites. Funnymen such as Jamie Foxx perform dead-on Cosby impressions at the drop of a hat. At the start of his career in the 1960s, Richard Pryor was trying to find his place among other comedians. He tried several approaches before settling on his edgy style. In his autobiography, *Pryor Convictions*, he talked about his early respect and admiration for Cosby:

> Bill Cosby was the guy who was most envied. I remember seeing a picture of Bill on the cover of *Time* magazine. Every comedian I knew had seen it and was jealous as an ugly whore. But Bill was good. Once when I played the Wha?, I heard Bill was at the Cellar, and so in between sets I went over to see his work for myself. . . . That man was amazing. Truly amazing. Do you hear me? I was amazed. . . .
>
> I finally met Bill Cosby at Papa Hud's. There was no doubt in anyone's mind, he was on his way. Cosby was going to the top. You could have put every dollar you had on that number. But he was still nice to me. He advised me to find my own thing.

In his 1987 concert, *Raw*, Eddie Murphy did a Cosby imper-sonation when he recounted a call he got from Bill Cosby after his son Ennis came home from a Murphy show. While the act displayed Murphy's respect for Cosby's work, it also showed his dissatisfaction with Cosby's opinions of his show:

> I've been a big fan of Bill Cosby all my life. Never met the man before, but he called me up about a year ago and chastised me on the phone for being too dirty onstage. He thought he should call me up and tell me what comedy is all about. . . . So I ran in the house all excited to talk to Bill and picked up the phone and he said [imitating Bill], "I would like to talk to you about some of the things you're doing in your show. I have five children, four girls and one boy. And one day my son came in the house all excited and asked if he could have money to go and see your show. Now, if the child is smiling and asking for money for a ticket, I have to give him money for a ticket. . . . We give him the money for the ticket and he goes to the show. We wait in the living room for him to return and when he does, he has a look on his face like he heard some stuff that he's never heard before. You cannot say filth flarn filth in front of people." . . . I got mad because he thought that was my whole act, like I just walked out onstage and just cursed and left. I managed to stick in some jokes between the curses.

While Murphy had problems with Cosby, other comics and entertainers were singing his praises. Jeff Foxworthy, a comic and game show host, shared his list of influences in a January 1995 article in *Entertainment Weekly*. Bill Cosby was his "No. 1 influence," he said, "because he was able to do comedy clean. Part of the art of comedy is finding a way to say things without being dirty. I think it's lazy, otherwise."

Bill Cosby performs during a segment on the *Late Show with David Letterman* in New York City, on June 1, 2009.

Chris Rock, whose edgy and intelligent comedy has made him one of the most successful comics today, fondly recalled Cosby's work. In the HBO Documentary Films presentation *The Black List: Volume One*, Chris said: "I have a picture in one of my offices of Cosby. It's a young Cosby with a fedora and a cigar. It's as cool as they come. My daughter Lola goes to sleep with a Little Bill doll. That's so cool, how much I love Cosby."

The love doesn't stop there. Quirky comic Doug E. Doug worked with Cosby on the CBS show *Cosby*. The two actors hit it off immediately. Doug's youthful physical comedy and offbeat humor suited Cosby's gruff character perfectly. In a November 17, 1996, article for the *New York Times*, Doug recounted his first meeting with Bill and his influence on his career. "It was a get-to-know-you meeting," Doug said, "but for me, it became a babble-and-slobber meeting. Why? Because Bill Cosby is my primary creative influence." The young comic also discussed his reaction to listening to Cosby's records as a child. "What I understood I laughed at, and what I didn't understand I still laughed at. I wanted to be just like him, and be able to make people laugh even at stuff they didn't quite understand." Other comics who cite Cosby as an influence and inspiration include Billy Crystal and Jerry Seinfeld.

In 2009, the Kennedy Center honored Bill Cosby by presenting him with the Mark Twain Prize for American Humor. Cosby often has said that the great American author was a big influence on his approach to comedy. Upon learning of his selection for the honor, Cosby issued a statement about his selection for the Twain Prize. "After bathing us, dressing us in fresh pajamas, and setting us into the crib together, Anna Pearl Cosby read to my brother James and me *The Adventures of Tom Sawyer*, and later, *The Adventures of Huckleberry Finn*," said Cosby. "I would like to apologize to Mr. Twain for falling asleep hundreds of times, but he should understand that I was only four."

Bill Cosby is a master comedian whose achievements will go unmatched for years to come. But his legacy is about more than just his skills as an entertainer or his work as a humanitarian. His life demonstrates that anyone can beat the odds through determination, education, hard work, and the willingness to learn and do as much as one can. That is a legacy he can certainly be proud of.

TELEVISION SHOWS AND APPEARANCES

1963, 1964 *The Tonight Show*; *That Was the Week That Was*

1965–1968 *I Spy*

1969–1971 *The Bill Cosby Show*

1971–1973 *The Electric Company*

1972–1973 *The New Bill Cosby Show*

1972–1977 *Fat Albert and the Cosby Kids*

1976 *Cos*

1979 *The New Fat Albert Show*

1984–1992 *The Cosby Show*

1987–1993 *A Different World* (executive producer)

1992–1993 *You Bet Your Life*

1992–1993 *Here and Now* (executive producer)

1994–1995 *The Cosby Mysteries*

1996–2000 *Cosby*

TV SPECIALS

1968 *The Bill Cosby Special*

1969 *The Second Bill Cosby Special*

1970 *The Third Bill Cosby Special*

1971 *The Bill Cosby Special, Or?*

1972 *Dick van Dyke Meets Bill Cosby*

1975 *Cos: The Bill Cosby Comedy Special*

1977 *The Fat Albert Halloween Special*; *The Fat Albert Christmas Special*

1984 *Johnny Carson Presents The Tonight Show Comedians*

1986 *Funny*

FILMS

1972   *Hickey and Boggs; Man and Boy*

1974   *Uptown Saturday Night*

1975   *Let's Do It Again*

1976   *Mother, Jugs & Speed*

1977   *A Piece of the Action*

1978   *California Suite*

1981   *The Devil and Max Devlin*

1982   *Bill Cosby: Himself*

1987   *Leonard Part 6*

1990   *Ghost Dad*

1993   *Meteor Man*

MADE-FOR-TV MOVIES

1971   *To All My Friends on Shore*

1978   *Top Secret*

1994   *I Spy Returns*

BOOKS

1973   *The Wit and Wisdom of Fat Albert*

1975   *Bill Cosby's Personal Guide to Tennis Power*

1986   *Fatherhood*

1988   *Time Flies*

1989   *Love and Marriage*

1991   *Childhood*

1997   *The Meanest Thing to Say: A Little Bill Book for Beginning Readers* (with Varnette P. Honeywood); *The Best Way to Play* (with Varnette P. Honeywood); *The Treasure Hunt* (with Varnette P. Honeywood)

1998 *Super-Fine Valentine* (with Varnette P. Honeywood); *Money Troubles* (with Varnette P. Honeywood)

1999 *Congratulations! Now What?: A Book for Graduates*

2001 *Cosbyology: Essays and Observations from the Doctor of Comedy*

2007 *Come On, People: On the Path from Victims to Victors* (with Alvin F. Poussaint)

RECORDINGS

1963 *Bill Cosby Is a Very Funny Fellow Right!*

1964 *I Started Out as a Child*

1965 *Why Is There Air?*

1966 *Wonderfulness*

1967 *Revenge*

1968 *To Russell, My Brother, Whom I Slept With*

1969 *Bill Cosby*

1970 *Live at Madison Square Garden*

1971 *When I Was a Kid*

1973 *Fat Albert*

1976 *Bill Cosby Is Not Himself These Days—Rat Own, Rat Own, Rat Own*

1990 *Where You Lay Your Head*

1997 *Hello Friend: To Ennis with Love*

1937 William Henry Cosby Jr. is born to Anna Pearl and William Cosby on July 12 in Philadelphia, Pennsylvania.

1956–1960 Cosby serves in the U.S. Navy medical corps. He also completes high school.

1961 He earns a track scholarship to Temple University in Philadelphia.

1963 He releases his first comedy album, *Bill Cosby is a Very Funny Fellow Right!* The recording receives a Grammy nomination.

1964 He marries Camille Olivia Hanks on January 25.

Cosby wins the first of six consecutive Grammy Awards for Best Comedy Recording for *I Started Out as a Child.*

1965 His daughter, Erika Ranee Cosby, is born. *I Spy* premiers.

1967 His daughter, Erinn Charlene Cosby, is born.

1969 His son, Ennis William Cosby, is born. Bill also stars in the NBC sitcom *The Bill Cosby Show.*

1972 He hosts the CBS variety series *The New Bill Cosby Show.*

1972–1985 He creates and hosts the animated CBS Saturday morning series *Fat Albert and the Cosby Kids.* The title was later changed to *The New Fat Albert and the Cosby Kids.*

1973 His daughter, Ensa Camille Cosby, is born.

1974 Cosby starts to work as a commercial spokesman for such products as Jell-O, Kodak, and Coca-Cola.

He acts in *Uptown Saturday Night,* directed by Sidney Poitier.

1976 He hosts the short-lived ABC variety series *Cos;* Cosby writes the dissertation *An Integration of the Visual Media via "Fat Albert and The Cosby Kids" Into the Elementary School Curriculum as a Teaching Aid and Vehicle to Achieve Increased Learning.*

1977 His daughter, Evin Harrah Cosby, is born.

1984   Bill creates and stars in the NBC sitcom *The Cosby Show* as Heathcliff Huxtable.

1986   He headlines the successful comedy show *An Evening with Bill Cosby* at New York City's Radio City Music Hall.

1989   Bill makes a $20 million donation to Spelman College in Atlanta, Georgia.

1990   Cosby stars in the film *Ghost Dad.*

1991   Bill receives an NAACP Image Award for Outstanding Actor in a Comedy Series (*The Cosby Show*).

1992   He hosts the syndicated revival of the 1950s game show *You Bet Your Life.* He is inducted into the TV Hall of Fame, Academy of Television Arts and Sciences. The final season of *The Cosby Show* airs.

1994   Cosby reunites with Robert Culp for the CBS TV movie *I Spy Returns.* He stars in the short-lived NBC series *The Cosby Mysteries.*

1996   Cosby stars in the CBS show *Cosby*, which also features former *Cosby Show* costar Phylicia Rashad.

1997   As a result of son Ennis' murder, the Cosbys announce the creation of the Hello Friend/Ennis William Cosby Foundation. The charitable organization addresses the early detection and treatment of dyslexia. Cosby releases the first three books of his *Little Bill* series for early readers.

1998   Bill hosts the CBS series *Kids Say the Darndest Things.* He receives an honorary degree from USC School of Cinema-Television. He also receives a Kennedy Center Honors Lifetime Achievement Award.

1999   Cosby becomes part owner of the New Jersey Nets pro basketball team.

2000   He receives an honorary degree from Fashion Institute of Technology (FIT).

2006   Cosby travels the country discussing education, parenting, and social responsibility in a program called *A Call
Out with Cosby.*

2008   Bill records the hip-hop CD titled *Cosby Narratives
Vol.1: State of Emergency.*

Adams, Barbara Johnston. *The Picture Life of Bill Cosby.* New York: F. Watts, 1986.

Adler, Bill. *The Cosby Wit: His Life and Humor.* New York: Carroll & Graf, 1986.

Bogle, Donald. *Blacks in American Films and Television: An Encyclopedia.* New York: Fireside, 1988.

———. *Primetime Blues: African Americans on Network Television.* New York: Farrar, Straus and Giroux, 2001.

Cohen, Joel H. *Cool Cos: The Story of Bill Cosby.* New York: Scholastic, 1969.

Haskins, James. *Bill Cosby, America's Most Famous Father.* New York: Walker & Company, 1988.

———. *The March on Washington.* New York: HarperCollins, 1993.

Littleton, Darryl. *Black Comedians on Black Comedy: How African-Americans Taught Us to Laugh.* New York: Applause Theatre & Cinema Books, 2006.

Rochelle, Belinda. *Witnesses to Freedom: Young People Who Fought for Civil Rights.* New York: Puffin, 1993.

Ruth, Marianne. *Bill Cosby.* Los Angeles: Melrose Square, 1992.

Smith, Ronald L. *Cosby: The Life of a Comedy Legend.* Amherst, N.Y.: Prometheus Books, 1997.

WEB SITES

Bill Cosby's Official Web Site
http://www.billcosby.com

Black Comics
http://www.listofblackcomedians.com

Comedy Peace Organization
http://www.comedy4peace.org

World Comedy Network: Comedy Guide and Calendar
http://www.worldcomedynetwork.com

Index

A freelance writer who has written about business, education, entertainment, human interest, beauty, and interior design, **Sonya Kimble-Ellis** is the author of the children's activity books *Math Puzzlers* and *Traditional African American Arts & Activities*. Her work has appeared in Scholastic's classroom magazines, *Black Enterprise*, the *New York Daily News*, *Celebrity Hairstyles*, and *Black Issues Book Review*, among other publications. She attended Rutgers University (Douglass College), where she majored in English. She lives in New Jersey with her husband, Michael. She gives special thanks to Ashley Bryant for her assistance with this project.